MEMORY
MAKERS

SCHOOL DAYS
Scrapbooks

Ideas, Tips & Techniques for
Scrapbooking the Grade School Years

M
MEMORY
MAKERS
BOOKS

DENVER, COLORADO

SAMANTHA, KINDERGARTEN

BOOK DIRECTORS   *Michele & Ron Gerbrandt*
EDITORIAL DIRECTOR   *MaryJo Regier*
ART DIRECTOR   *Karen Roehl*
CRAFT DIRECTOR   *Pam Klassen*
ASSOCIATE EDITOR   *Kimberly Ball*
IDEA EDITOR   *Janetta Wieneke*
STAFF ARTIST   *Pamela Frye*
PHOTOGRAPHER   *Ken Trujillo*
PHOTO STYLIST   *Sylvie Abecassis*
CONTRIBUTING PHOTOGRAPHERS   *Liz Campanella, Brenda Martinez*
CONTRIBUTING DESIGNERS   *Tracy Heller, Susha Roberts, Pia Valeriana*
CONTRIBUTING WRITERS   *Kelly Angard, Sharon Ball, Heath McKenny, Heather McWhorter, Margaret Radford, Lori Elkins Solomon*
CONTRIBUTING ARTISTS   *Kelly Angard, Alison Beachem, Lorna Dee Christensen, Brandi Ginn, Ann Kitayama, Pam Metzger, Stacey Shigaya, Debby Schuh*
PATTERN ILLUSTRATIONS   *Sarah Daniels*
LETTERING ARTISTS   *Joy Carey, Lorna Dee Christensen, Jennifer Pond*
EDITORIAL SUPPORT   *Jennifer St. Onge, Dena Twinem*

Memory Makers® School Days Scrapbooks
Copyright © 2002 Memory Makers Books
All rights reserved.

Published by Memory Makers Books,
an imprint of F & W Publications, Inc.
12365 Huron Street, Suite 500, Denver, CO 80234
Phone 1-800-254-9124
First edition. Printed in the United States.

06 05 04 03 02   5 4 3 2 1

Library of Congress Cataloging-in-Publication Data

Memory Makers school days scrapbooks : ideas, tips & techniques for scrapbooking the
grade school years.-- 1st ed.
    p. cm.
  Includes bibliographical references and index.
  ISBN 1-892127-17-2
   1. Photograph albums. 2. Photographs--Conservation and restoration. 3. Scrapbooks. 4.
School children--Collectibles. I. Title: School days scrapbooks. II. Memory makers.

TR465 .M475 2002
745.593--dc21

            2002067754

Distributed to trade and art markets by
F & W Publications, Inc.
4700 East Galbraith Road, Cincinnati, OH 45236
Phone 1-800-289-0963

ISBN 1-89212-717-2

Memory Makers Books is the home of *Memory Makers*, the scrapbook magazine dedicated to educating
and inspiring scrapbookers. To subscribe, or for more information, call 1-800-366-6465.
Visit us on the Internet at www.memorymakersmagazine.com

THIS BOOK BELONGS TO

_____

We dedicate this book to all of our Memory Makers
contributors whose fun and creative projects, albums
and ideas are the inspiration behind these pages.

Contents

7   INTRODUCTION

8   GETTING STARTED

13   PHOTO, MEMORABILIA AND JOURNALING
      CHECKLISTS

14   Back to School
      Back-to-school shopping madness project page,
      back to school, wake up, getting ready, school
      bus, Pledge of Allegiance project page, reliev-
      ing first day jitters, first day of school, pocket
      page ideas, preserving memorabilia

34   All in a Day's Work
      Artwork, homework, best-beloved books about school
      for grades K-6, summer school, classes, a typical school day
      from a child's perspective, lunch, recess, friends, science fair,
      special class projects, school days punch art
      page and borders

50   HOME SCHOOLING
      Page ideas and scrapbooking tips for home-schoolers

54   Activities & Special Events

56   SPORTS
      Baseball, football, basketball and soccer page ideas; photograph-
      ing memorabilia; sports theme album; flip photos page idea

61   PERFORMANCES
      Musicals, stage plays, dancing and recital page ideas

64   CLUBS & ACTIVITIES
      4-H, clubs and scouting page ideas

PAGE 15

68   FIELD TRIPS
Field trip page ideas

72   CELEBRATIONS
Class parties and special events page ideas, party theme album

80   FIELD DAYS
Field day page ideas

82   AWARDS & CEREMONIES
Achievement page ideas

84   GRADUATION
Graduation page ideas

88   Portraits & Milestones
Class and individual portraits page ideas, big uses for
small portraits, adding eyelets technique, enlisting your
child's help to make photo mats, paper folding technique, working with heritage photos, paper silhouettes
technique, referencing group photos technique, portrait
album, helping your child build confidence, timelines,
year-in-review fold-out page, student & teacher appreciation albums, gift bag, last day of school page ideas

104   DOCUMENTING THE DIFFICULT TIMES
Moving, autism, attention deficit disorder progress
page ideas

116   QUOTES & SAYINGS

118   LETTERING PATTERNS & PAGE TITLE IDEAS

120   PROJECT & PAPER PIECING PATTERNS

122   PAGE PATTERNS

125   INSTRUCTIONS, CREDITS & SOURCES

128   INDEX

PAGE 41

OUR LITTLE ARTISTS

Sasha - Kindergarten

Daniel - 1ST grade

Each of our children loves to create their own masterpieces. Painting and drawing are an important part of our lives.

Anna - 2nd grade

Introduction

Each year, as summer winds down and my children and I head out for the "back-to-school" shopping experience, it is easy to get caught up in the excitement and anticipation that a new school year brings and the memories of school days gone by. My earliest grade school memory goes back to kindergarten. I vividly remember walking to school and clanging my metal lunch box against my knees while waiting with a group of kids for the crossing guard to allow us to cross the street. I couldn't wait to get to class and be with my teacher.

Children have a natural love of learning, and as much as school life has changed since I was in school, some things remain constant. Who can forget the pride of owning your very own, shiny backpack and sharpened pencils for the first time? And remember wondering who would sit next to you and the aroma of food wafting down the hallway from the cafeteria, making your stomach grumble?

Some things you just never forget as your senses rush over you and the mental images replay. However, the details of such important events can fade over time. When you preserve your or your children's school memories and activities, it is easy to reminisce by simply flipping through the pages of a unique scrapbook album.

In this book, we provide countless page ideas to help you document all of the hard work, the triumphs and the tribulations, the opportunities and the special details that capture the essence of grade school. We've included ideas for everything—from back-to-school experiences, daily school life, activities and special events to home schooling, documenting the difficult times and unique treatments for school portraits. In addition, we feature fun techniques, original paper piecing patterns, reproducible page patterns and more to help you get started. You'll also get to hear from kids who are creating their own scrapbooks. Maybe their stories will inspire your own grade-schooler to start scrapping.

One thing is certain. At no other time in a child's education will more school papers, photographs, and memorabilia come home than in grade school—each item with its own unique story to tell. I hope this book will inspire you with new pages to create and photographs to take. With these great ideas, your school days pages are guaranteed to make the grade!

Michele

MICHELE GERBRANDT
FOUNDER OF *MEMORY MAKERS*® MAGAZINE

OUR LITTLE ARTISTS
(SEE PAGE 125)

1 Getting Started

The years spent in school are very busy, packed with many memorable moments, events, friendships and accomplishments you don't want to forget. Ideally, you could do your school scrapbooking as it happens and as your child grows. Unfortunately, that is not the case for most of us. Therefore, some organization and planning are essential. Here are some easy steps to help you get started.

1 Set Up a Work Area

Your work area should have a level work surface, good lighting and good access to your scrapbooking supplies, photos and other memorabilia. Preferably this is an area you can leave and come back to without much time spent on setup or cleanup. You may also want to make sure you are near an electrical outlet, especially if you use a light box, embossing gun, extra lighting or computer.

2 Decide on a Format

Decide how much information you want to include for each grade. Remember that the amount of information you choose to use will have a direct result on the size and the amount of time you spend on the scrapbook. If you're a scrapbooker who likes to scrap everything, you may want to consider dividing your school scrapbook into two or three separate scrapbooks (primary and secondary or elementary, middle and high school).

3 Create Categories

Write categories for your photos and memorabilia on sticky notes. Categories can be in chronological order, by theme or even modeled after the chapters in this book. See the photos and memorabilia checklists on page 13 for ideas. You can add or remove categories as you go.

4 Organize Photos & Memorabilia

Good organization is key to being successful in your scrapbooking. Try to store and save all school photos and memorabilia in the same area of your home. This eliminates wasting time trying to remember which shelf, box or closet holds which photos. It is important to try to label or make notes about photos as soon as possible. Jot details on sticky notes or on the backs of photos with a photo-safe wax pencil. This will help prevent forgetting special moments and will assist you when it's time to journal.

5 Store Photos & Negatives

Any time you put this much time and effort into something as special as your child's scrapbook, it deserves the added effort of making sure it will last. Store extra photos and negatives in archival quality binders, boxes and sleeves to help secure your memories for future generations.

SCISSORS & PAPER TRIMMER

Keep a pair of sharp, straight-edge scissors and a paper trimmer at hand. Also, use decorative scissors for creative edges on photos and mats. Turn decorative scissors over to achieve a varied cutting pattern.

2 Basic Tools & Supplies

Once you've chosen a format and organized your photos and memorabilia, you're almost ready to create your first page. But first, gather the following tools:

ADHESIVES

Use scrapbooking adhesives, such as glues, tapes and mounting corners, that are labeled "acid-free" and "photo-safe." Rubber cement, white school glue and cellophane tape contain chemicals that can harm photos over time.

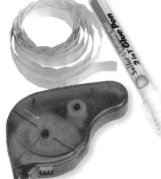

PAPERS

Acid- and lignin-free decorative papers are available in countless colors and patterns. Use these versatile papers for a background, an accent, or to mat or frame photos.

ALBUMS

Albums come in strap-style, three-ring binder or post-bound, allowing you to remove, add, or rearrange pages as needed. Spiral-bound albums make great theme albums for children or gift albums. The quantity and physical size of your photos and memorabilia will help determine the size of album you need.

DESIGN ADDITIONS

Unique design additions can give a page theme continuity. These can include stickers, die cuts, memorabilia pockets, photo corners and more. Shop with a list of needed supplies and some photos to match colors and avoid any unnecessary spending.

RULERS & TEMPLATES

Use rulers and templates to crop photos or trace shapes onto paper, to cut decorative photo mats or to create your own die cuts.

PENCILS, PENS & MARKERS

Journaling adds the voice and pertinent facts to your scrapbook. A rainbow of journaling pens and markers, with a variety of pen tips, make penmanship a snap. Pigment ink pens are best because of their permanence.

3 Create a Layout

FOCAL POINT

Choose an enlarged, matted, unique or exceptional photo for a focal point on the page to help determine an eye-pleasing layout. This is where the eye will look first. Other photos on the page should support this image.

BALANCE

Place your photos on a one- or two-page spread. Large, bright or busy photos can feel "heavier" than others, so move the photos around until the page no longer feels weighted or lopsided. Remember to leave enough space for journaling.

COLOR

Choose background and photo mat papers and design additions that complement the photos, making them stand out rather than compete for attention. Sometimes less is more. Too much color can be distracting.

4 Crop-n-Assemble

CROPPING

Photo cropping (Figure 1) can add style, emphasize a subject or remove a busy background. See *Memory Makers Creative Photo Cropping for Scrapbooks* for hundreds of cropping ideas.

MATTING

Single or layered paper photo mats focus attention and add balance to a page. Use a paper trimmer (Figure 2), decorative scissors, a template or freehand cut a mat, leaving a border around the photo.

MOUNTING

Mount photos on your page with double-sided tape (Figure 3) or liquid adhesives for a permanent bond. Paper or plastic photo corner triangles allow for easy removal of photos, if needed.

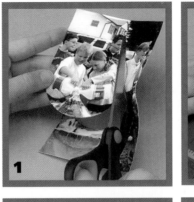
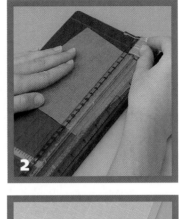

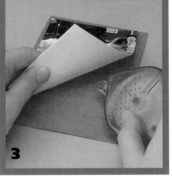

5 Journaling

The stories behind the photos are details that can be lost forever if they're not included on your page. Start with one, or a combination, of these simple journaling styles:

JOURNALING TIPS

- Write freehand in light pencil first, then trace with ink.
- Journal on a separate piece of paper (Figure 4), cut it out and mount it on the page.
- Use a pencil to trace a lettering or journaling template on the page, then trace with ink.
- Print journaling on your computer. Crop, mat and mount journaling or trace the journaling onto your page using a light box.
- Journal onto die cuts or mats, write around your photos in curved lines or turn paragraphs into shapes.
- Photocopy and color the lettering patterns on pages 118-119 for quick page titles.
- Use the journaling checklist on page 13 to help bring your photographic story to life.

STORYTELLING

Give details about those in the photo at the time the photo was taken. Include everything from clothing, background items, mood, and conversation—perhaps even the weather!

QUOTES, POEMS & SAYINGS

Search for your subject on quote-related Web sites, in poetry books, in the Bible, even on T-shirts! Or write your own.

BULLETS

List the basics of who, what, when and where in bullet form.

CAPTIONS

Expand on bulleted information with complete sentences, allowing for more creative expression.

- Leah, age 11
- 6th Grade
- Science: studying volcanoes
- Community Christian School
- 2001

Volcano! Leah made an erupting papier-mâché volcano for 6th grade science. Community Christian School Age 11 2001

There once was a girl named Leah
Who just couldn't wait to be a
Science class whiz
Her volcano did fizz
And everyone yelled, "Mama Mia!"

Community
Christian School
2001
6th Grade
age 11

science project

6th grade

Leah's 6th grade class worked in pairs to make papier-mâché volcanoes. The kids' vinegar, baking soda and food-coloring concoctions made for great eruptions! The kids learned that teamwork leads to success. The whole school loved this project! Community Christian School, 2001   Age 11

Teams: (left to right) Traci and Leah Jason and Alexia, Brittany and Ian with Sara watching, Brandon and Chris with Levi watching.

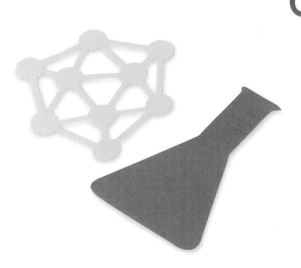

6 The Complete Page

It's easy to get caught up in the avalanche of scrap-booking products available, but it's important to stay focused on the purpose of scrapbooking when completing a page—to preserve your memories. With that in mind, make sure your page has the five basic elements of a great scrapbook page: photos, journaling, complementary color, effective design and long-lasting construction.

Photos Dawn Brough, Broomfield, Colorado
Design Pam Klassen, Broomfield, Colorado

Checklists

Throughout your child's school years, you'll gather lots of photos and memorabilia that you'll want to preserve. Use these lists to help collect and organize memorabilia for your school days scrapbook.

PHOTOS

- Individual portraits
- Class portraits
- Favorite teachers
- Best friends
- Growth
- Favorite things
- What I learned
- First day of school
- Last day of school
- Field trips
- Doing homework
- Special school clothes
- School building

- Daily routine:
  - waking up
  - getting ready
  - catching the bus
  - class
  - lunch
  - recess
  - after-school activities
- Sports
- Scouting
- Performances
- Awards
- Science/Social Studies/ History/Math fair
- Field day
- Reading
- Studying

- Honors
- Class pets
- Fundraisers
- Recess
- School lunches
- Field trips or travels
- School carnivals or festivals
- Art, 4-H or other exhibitions
- Celebrations or holidays
- Snow days
- Pep rallies
- Community service
- Student council
- Talent show
- What I did over spring break

- What I did over summer break
- Teacher or student appreciation
- E-mail or pen pals
- Summer school
- What I want to be when I grow up
- Remembering a class-mate (In memory of)
- Graduations
- Your child with:
  - friends
  - teachers or principal
  - coaches
  - exchange students
  - family and siblings

JOURNALING

You can't go to school with your child, so make sure you ask them lots of questions or get them to journal themselves. Some things you might wish to record:

- Favorite things at a given age
- What your child learned in a given year
- How your child felt about teachers, classmates and classes
- First day of school mishaps
- Educational milestones and successes
- Your child's strengths and weaknesses
- What happened during the year? (world events)
- Information off school Web site
- School or club song, pledge, cheer or motto
- School rules or dress code
- Your child's growth
- Autographs from class-mates

- Some of your child's opinions
- Some of your child's quotes
- History of school or school mascot
- The funniest thing that happened in school
- Most embarrassing moment in school
- Best moment in school
- What is unique about your child?
- Personality and character traits of your child
- Why you are proud of your child
- Moving from elementary to middle school

MEMORABILIA

Keep the memorabilia that's important to your child and your child's elementary school experience. Consider photographing an overabundance of memorabilia for your album if necessary.

- Artwork
- Handwriting samples from each grade
- Copies of homework
- Certificates, ribbons and awards from organized activities
- Notes from classmates and teachers
- Pieces of projects
- Class schedule
- School supplies

- Copies of textbook covers
- Report Cards
- Special test scores
- Newspaper clippings
- School bumper stickers or pennants
- Programs or fliers from special events
- Meaningful doodles
- Handprints
- Receipts
- Ticket stubs
- Photocopy of school images, logos, pledges, etc.

Jake's Backpack

receipt
for all of Jake's backpack stuff

Jake starts school with his very own shiny
new supplies! It takes a big boy to handle
such a heavy backpack!
August 15,1996

Back to School

Some of our most powerful childhood memories are of those magical days when the lazy sweetness of summer gave way to the fresh-scrubbed structure of school. After all, getting ready is a happy shock to the senses: the fresh, woody smell of newly sharpened pencils; the crisp, orderly feel of folders and notebook paper; the sweaty adrenaline rush of shopping for the "cool" apparel; the tugs of combing through summer's tangles and the panic of searching for socks, much less socks that actually match. It's all worth it, though, when hand and heart come together for The Pledge of Allegiance and the first lessons of the school year. These are the times when both kids and parents will find endless possibilities—and endless memories to treasure and share.

"SCHOOLS DAYS, SCHOOL DAYS;

DEAR OLD GOLDEN RULE DAYS.

READIN' AND WRITIN' AND

'RITHMETIC; TAUGHT TO THE TUNE

OF A HICK'RY STICK."

—*Will D. Cobb (1876-1930)*

JAKE'S BACKPACK
(SEE PAGE 125)

LEROY DRIVE ELEMENTARY, 1ST GRADE

Once again this year, Allison and I went out for that annual mother-daughter bonding ritual, back-to-school shopping. Since time began (OK, or at least as far back as I can remember!), every August closets and drawers are purged of too-tight underwear, flood pants, and shirts with arms holes that pinch in preparation for the big day. On the morning of this year's shop-fest, Allison and I jumped out of bed early, threw on our walking shoes, and headed for the mall. We carefully constructed ensembles sure to transform Allison's juvenile 4th grade self into this year's sophisticated, glitter-wearing, cool 5th grader.

Annual Back-to-School
SHOPPING MADNESS!

Allison
age 10

Back-to-School Shopping Madness

OUTFIT AN ARMOIRE WITH SCHOOL CLOTHES

Kathleen took photos of her daughter's back-to-school shopping spree "finds" to create a two-page "room" spread complete with a stocked armoire of her own design—an idea that works equally well for both girls and boys. Like Kathleen, you may want to feature a combination of actual clothes and paper-pieced clothes in the armoire. First, follow the tips on page 17 for *Photographing for Proper Perspective* to take pictures of your child in different outfits. Then "wallpaper" the page backgrounds with floral and striped patterned papers (Colorbök); add floral sticker strips (Mary Engelbreit).

For the left page, triple mat computer-printed journaling and title block (Broderbund) and adhere. Decorate "room" with furniture punch-outs (Mary Engelbreit). Silhouette-crop and mat photo of child in classic modeling pose. For the right page, follow the steps on page 17 to create and assemble the armoire and the clothing to hang in it. Accent page with more punch-outs to complete the spread.

Kathleen Lindner, La Palma, California

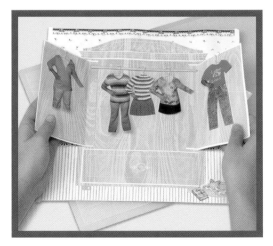

Photographing for Proper Perspective

Begin by photographing your child in a classic "modeling" pose, like the one Allison struck on the page at left. Use tape to mark the spot on the floor where your child stands for the first picture. Also mark where you are standing to take the pictures, thus ensuring that the same distance is between the two of you for all photos to gain equal perspective in all photos. Also, be sure that your child is posed the same in each photo. If her left arm is extended outward, as Allison is doing, be sure that her same arm is extended in all photos in the same manner.

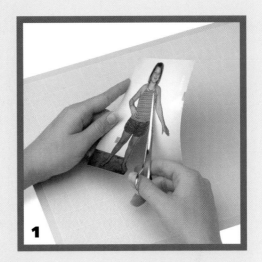

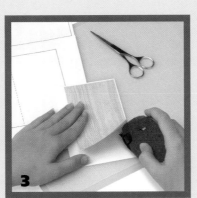

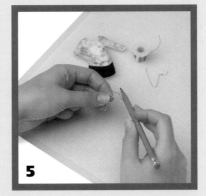

1 Use small, sharp scissors to silhouette-crop photos of child (Figure 1), staying true to the outline of the child and being careful not to lop off fingers, toes, hair and ears. Repeat with photos of child in different outfits, keeping just the outfits this time.

2 Copy and enlarge the armoire pattern on page 120, sizing to fit page and perspective of your child's photos; cut out pattern pieces. Trace around pattern pieces (Figure 2) onto wood-grain patterned paper (Provo Craft). Cut out wood grain pieces, cutting a tiny bit to the inside of the traced lines.

3 Adhere armoire doors (Figure 3) and lower drawer to white cardstock. Fold doors along dotted lines to form "hinge" on which you will mount doors onto dresser.

4 Using the photos on the opposite page as a guide, adhere the doors to armoire (Figure 4), then assemble remaining dresser components.

5 Grab an actual wire hanger from your closet to use as a guide; twist craft wire in the same fashion to create wire hangers (Figure 5) on which to hang "clothes."

Summer's end brings back the back-to-school shopping experience. It's an annual tradition that parents, and their wallets, have come to expect. But in 1993, that tradition came with a twist for Sabina's family. A family friend, who owned a children's clothing store, asked Sabina's permission for her children to pose in a newspaper ad and television commercial for the store. The event turned into a scrapbook page.

"I see this as an opportunity to remind my children of some of the neat things they got to do when they were young," she says. "Not every child gets to be in a TV or newspaper ad." After posing in the August heat for many shots and lots of videotape footage, the ads were completed and Sabina's kids were allowed to keep the new clothing.

"To me it's special because these are my children, but for future generations it will say a lot about our time, the style of dress for children and how items were promoted for sale," says Sabina.

Beyond the historical significance, she hopes her albums will have personal meaning for her descendants as well. "I love seeing photos of my ancestors when they were children," she says. "It gives me a glimpse of them that I might not otherwise have. I expect my albums to do the same for future generations."

Sabina Dougherty-Wiebkin, Lebanon, New Hampshire

Wake Up

PHOTOJOURNAL A "GETTING READY" PAGE

Joyce kept school mornings running smoothly by designing a "get ready for school" page and hanging it on her daughter's door during the school year. Begin by stamping (Stampendous) a colorful background design. Crop and mat photos into circles with decorative scissors (Creative Memories). Layer and overlap title letters (Creative Memories) and photos on page. Add clock clip art (source unknown) to complete.

Joyce Schweitzer, Greensboro, North Carolina

Back to School

CHRONICLE A MORNING ROUTINE

Kimberly remembers her kids' first day of school with photos documenting the morning's activities. Begin by mounting two 5" paper strips along left and right sides of page. Adhere sticker letters (Creative Memories). Crop photos using oval template (Creative Memories) and decorative scissors. Circle cut clock faces; mat with solid paper and detail with pens.

Kimberly Trachtman
Sharpsville, Pennsylvania

The Bus

PAPER-PIECE SCHOOL BUS FRAMES

Donna brings her twins' favorite song to life with a cleverly crafted school bus frame. Cut brown patterned paper (MPR Assoc.) into road shape; mount on plaid background paper (Provo Craft). Paper-piece freehand-cut bus shapes by cutting yellow arches, silver bumpers, black wheels and stripes, and red lights. Adhere sticker letters (Provo Craft) to red paper; trim around letters. Complete page with journaling and words to the song.

Donna Pittard, Kingwood, Texas

School Time

PEN CHALKBOARD PHOTO CORNERS

Heather shows her four boys traveling on the road to school with a collection of photos from their first day. Create background by layering 2½" strip of black cardstock trimmed along the top with decorative scissors (Fiskars); layer over patterned paper (NRN Designs). Punch large white rectangles (Family Treasures) for road lines; slice horizontally in half and mount on black road. Adhere crosswalk sticker (Frances Meyer); draw white post. Freehand draw and cut out school bus. Silhouette photos and layer; mount with self-adhesive foam spacers. Crop remaining photos; mat circle-cut photo on black cardstock square. Cut black photo corners; detail with white pen.

Heather Spurlock, Salt Lake City, Utah

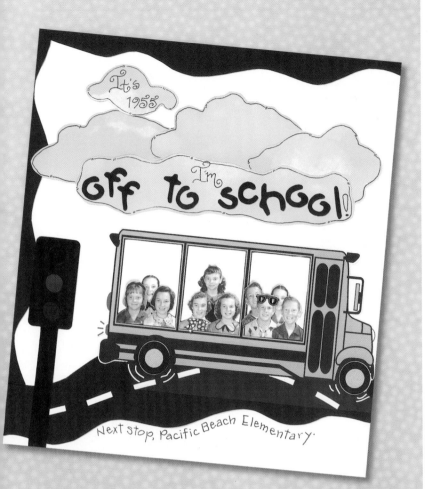

Off to School
TRANSPORT FRIENDS IN STYLE

Nadine created a clever school bus full of kids from vintage photos of her fifth-grade class. Begin by creating road and borders with decorative ruler (EK Success). Punch and halve white rectangles (Family Treasures) for road lines. Silhouette-crop school bus from patterned paper (Hot Off the Press); layer over road. Silhouette-crop "students" from copy of class photo; layer behind bus windows and add stickers (Mary Englebreit, Mrs. Grossman's). Mount red, gold and green metallic paper (Making Memories) scraps behind traffic signal die cut (Ellison) prior to mounting on page. Freehand cut clouds from patterned paper (source unknown). Adhere title sticker letters (Provo Craft) and complete journaling and cloud details with black pen.

Nadine Babbitt, San Diego, California

1st Day of Kindergarten
PHOTOGRAPH THE SCHOOL BUILDING

Rachel captured the excitement of her daughter's first day of school with classic first-day photos. Begin by cropping a large triangle with decorative scissors; mount on page. Craft school bus and chalkboard using a template (Provo Craft). Handcraft paper dolls; detail with pen and chalk. Mount dolls behind bus windows and adhere to page. Crop photos; round corners and mat. Adhere first day photo with black photo corners. Complete page with pen details and journaling.

Rachel Vezeau, Cary, Illinois

Stamping

Stamping lends a versatile and artistic touch to scrapbook pages, whether you stamp simple border designs or an entire background. The wide array of available stamp designs and ink colors makes it easy to create the perfect accent for school days pages, regardless of their theme.

I Pledge Allegiance

ACCENT A PATRIOTIC MOMENT

Stamping a red, white and blue background proved to be the perfect backdrop for photos of Julie's children, learning "The Pledge of Allegiance" from their father before school starts. Follow the steps below to stamp this background. Then create photo and journaling mats with a three-star corner slot punch (All Night Media); mount on page. Add punched and layered jumbo and small stars (Emagination Crafts); detail with pen strokes. Finish with stamped title (Stampin' Up!); color, mat and adhere.

Julie Swanson, South Milwaukee, Wisconsin

1 *In red ink, stamp double line stitch (Stampin' Up!) diagonally across page at 1" intervals. Repeat in blue ink starting at a different corner to create the crisscross pattern (Figure 1).*

2 *Apply color to stars and stripes of heart-shaped flag stamp (Stampin' Up!) with blue and red stamping markers (Stampin' Up!) as shown (Figure 2).*

3 *Stamp background in the squares that are created by the crisscross pattern (Figure 3) of the line stamping.*

Your First Day of Kindergarten

PUNCH A TITLE BLOCK

Sally reflects on her daughter's first day of kindergarten with a wonderful story to remember, accented by a punched title block. Crop and mat photo using corner rounder. Adhere crayon stickers (Frances Meyer) for border; draw black lines. Punch small red apples (Marvy/Uchida); trim off stems and layer on page as shown. Draw letters, stems and leaves, highlights and rest of title with pens. Complete page with journaling.

Sally Scamfer, Bellevue, Nebraska

Phyllis' Story

"When I first started writing about the memory of my daughter's school bus ride on her first day of kindergarten, I couldn't get past the picture of that tiny little girl stretching up so far to reach the first step," says Phyllis. "A box of tissues was gone before I could finally continue with my work. There is definitely a therapeutic element to this hobby!"

Phyllis Dollman, Culpeper, Virginia

RELIEVING FIRST-DAY JITTERS FOR CHILDREN AND THEIR PARENTS

The first day of school is a long-anticipated occasion. But mixed in with the excitement is often a lot of anxiety—not only for children, but for parents as well. Avoid first-day jitters by doing a little "homework" before the first day of school.

• Take your child on a tour of the school and, if possible, introduce her to the teacher, principal and other key adults.

• If your child will be taking a school bus, find out if you and your child can take a trial run on the bus before the first day of school. If your child will walk, practice following the route to and from school.

• Organize a get-together with other families in the neighborhood whose children attend the school so your child can get to know future schoolmates.

• Plan a fun after-school activity to do with your child so she has something to look forward to even if she has a tough first day.

• Read a book or watch a video about school, and talk about the characters' experiences with your child.

• Set a good example by staying calm and appearing confident. Children look to adults as role models. If you act nervous and tearful, so will your child. If you have a positive outlook, your child will have one as well.

• Play school. Set up a desk and chalkboard, and take turns assuming the roles of teacher and student.

• "Early to bed and early to rise" really will help a child to succeed. At least one week before school starts, change your child's sleep schedule. Well-rested children tend to be less anxious.

• Go shopping. Let your child select a back-to-school outfit that he or she will look forward to wearing on the first day of class. (Be sure to check the school's dress code beforehand!)

• Tuck encouraging notes and goodies into your child's backpack and lunch bag to give her a confidence boost during the day.

Will Does Kindergarten

ADD A MINI JOURNALING ALBUM

The special feature of Susan's spread is a handmade mini spiral album that features lots of space for journaling. To begin, layer patterned (Provo Craft) and wood-grain stamped paper (Coop Stamps) with solid paper for background. Freehand cut, crimp, punch and assemble schoolhouse; add pen stroke details. Cut schoolhouse in half and adhere to center of spread. Cut grass border with decorative scissors (Provo Craft) and stamp (All Night Media); adhere in front of schoolhouse. Use a ⅛" round hand punch to punch holes around edges of pages; insert cording and tie off on back of pages. Crop, mat and layer photos across spread, accenting photo mats with stamped designs (All Night Media, Inkadinkado, Judikins, Posh Impressions, Rubber Stampede, Stamps "N" Memories, Toomuchfun Rubberstamps) on mats, corner triangles and squares. Freehand cut apple; stamp leaves (Stampin' Up!), crimp stem and add photo. Add school bus picture frame and stickers (Creative Imaginations). For title, mat letter stickers (Provo Craft), accent "kindergarten" die cut (Memories Forever) with white ink, lace with more cording and insert freehand cut and drawn pencils. To make flag, cut ¼" strips of red and white paper; adhere to paper rectangle with punched square (Family Treasures) and stars (McGill). Crimp whole flag; cut rectangle into blocks and adhere with blocks set slightly askew. Follow instructions to the right to make the mini spiral album. Journal in album and accent with cropped photos and stickers to complete.

Susan Badgett, North Hills, California

To make mini spiral album, crop cardstock "book" using one color for cover and another color for interior pages. Punch ⅛" circles every ¼" along the "binding" of cardstock book. Place a kabob skewer or an embossing stylus atop binding holes; wrap craft wire around skewer and weave through the punched holes to create spiral. Hide the wire ends behind the booklet before mounting on page.

Kindergarten

1997 * 1998

Cady Wendt

A Bit Of Cody's

Handiwork

Kindergarten

FEATURE STUDENT'S SCHOOLWORK

Gretchen loves to save samples of her stepson's schoolwork without having many papers to file, so she reduces them on a copy machine and creates a coordinating layout. For photo mat, layer patterned paper (The Paper Patch) over solid, leaving ¼" border for the background. Mat portrait on patterned paper; trim solid paper with decorative scissors (Fiskars). Adhere yellow sticker strips around photo. Add sticker letters (Provo Craft) to matted title blocks. Mount scissors die cut (Ellison). Double mat child's autograph; accent with pencil sticker (Mrs. Grossman's). Color photocopy and reduce school papers; mat on solid paper.

Gretchen Wendt, Once Upon a Time
St. John, Indiana

School days scrapbooks would not be the same without ribbons, certificates, programs, receipts and more to personalize the pages. Follow the tips below to help preserve memorabilia.

• Assume that all memorabilia you wish to add to your scrapbook is acidic; don't let memorabilia and photos touch.

• De-acidify newspaper clippings and announcements with Archival Mist™ (Preservation Technologies).

• Use PVC-free memorabilia protectors to encapsulate memorabilia before mounting on page.

• Consider using a photograph of the memorabilia as an alternative to mounting actual memorabilia, thus reducing added bulk in your scrapbook album.

School Days

USE A READY-MADE POCKET

An old manila folder made a perfect pocket for Joy's kindergarten memorabilia. Spray folder and memorabilia with Archival Mist™ (Preservation Technologies); mount folder with clear photo corners and insert memorabilia. Crop photo and mat on solid paper; freehand cut apple. Design title art (Provo Craft) with pen and watercolors. Write subtitle letters with template (Pebbles In My Pocket) and white pen. Add journaling.

Joy Carey, Visalia, California

Kindergarten

CREATE A QUICK-AND-EASY POCKET PAGE

Janna created a simple pocket page to hold her daughter's kindergarten memorabilia. Begin the quick-and-easy pocket by adhering an "overall" (EK Success) to yellow cardstock; trim top into wavy design as shown. Slice four ½" strips of red cardstock; mount around edges of "pocket" and at bottom of overall where it overlaps yellow cardstock. Turn page pocket over; apply adhesive to sides and lower edge, leaving the top open to form pocket. Mount pocket on patterned paper background (Me & My Big Ideas). Mat and mount photos and title (EK Success). Adhere stickers (Mrs. Grossman's), silhouette-cropped crayons and face (EK Success). Complete page with journaling and pen strokes on photo mats.

Janna Wilson, Rudy, Arkansas

First Day of School

STAMP A SCHOOL-THEME BORDER

Michele's selection of primary colors and school-theme stamps reflects the excitement of her kindergartner's first day of school. Stamp designs (Close To My Heart) on white paper; color with pens and chalk. Cut and mat 2¾" tall borders with decorative scissors; mount on printed background paper (Close To My Heart). Print title and text block; chalk edges. Double mat and trim with decorative scissors. Mat again; detail with pen strokes. Crop photos and mat, adding freehand cut paper corners to highlight largest photo.

Michele Rank
Cerritos, California

On 9/7/00 Zachary went to his first day of kindergarten. His school is Benito Juarez Elementary School, and it is right around the corner from our house. His teacher is Mrs. Arbouin and he is in class number A-3. There are 20 classmates for Zach to get to know. School starts at 8:40 AM and he gets out at 1:25 PM. Lunchtime at school is at 11:45. To prepare for kindergarten Zachary got to pick out a brand new Backpack & supplies, lunchbox and clothes. As a special treat for starting school Zachary got to a special gift, lunch at McDonald's lunch & a toy monster trucks. When I picked up Zach from his first day of school, he would not stop talking about his new friends and how much fun he had. We are sure Zach will thrive in his new school.

First Day of School

COORDINATE BORDER WITH PHOTO MATS

Kelly combined a variety of border stickers (Me & My Big Ideas) to coordinate with photos matted with patterned paper. Begin by cropping photos; double and triple mat on solid and patterned (The Paper Patch) papers. Print text; double mat on solid and patterned (Provo Craft) papers. Adhere title and school-theme stickers (Me & My Big Ideas) on white paper; silhouette and layer on page.

Kelly Angard, Highlands Ranch, Colorado

My First Day

ADD DETAIL WITH POETIC JOURNALING

A poem becomes the perfect title and caption for Melissa's daughter's first-day photos. Print poem and crop photos; mat on solid paper. Mount die cut (My Mind's Eye) on solid paper; trim to size. Adhere all pieces on patterned paper (The Paper Patch).

Melissa Rhoads, Nibley, Utah

First Grade

SILHOUETTE CROP A STAMPED BORDER

Oksanna stamped and silhouette-cropped a bushel of apples to frame photos of her first-grader's special day on a crisp, two-page spread. Begin background design by trimming patterned (Frances Meyer) paper to 7¼ x 9¾" with decorative scissors (Fiskars); mount on pages atop patterned paper (Frances Meyer) as shown.

For upper page, use decorative corner punch (Fiskars) to create photo mat; insert double-matted photo trimmed with decorative scissors (Fiskars).

For lower page, cut journaling block; use corner rounder punch and add swirl border punch (All Night Media) after journaling with gold pen. Mat on patterned paper; adhere to page. Circle crop second photo; double mat on patterned and solid paper and adhere to page.

For both pages, mount stamped and silhouette-cropped apples around border. Complete pages with title letters cut from templates (Accu-Cut, C-Thru Ruler); mount as shown. Add swirl punch (All Night Media) details to letters and dragonfly punch (EK Success) for date at bottom of page.

Oksanna Pope
Los Gatos, California

Postcard from Mrs. Timin

Savannah 2nd & Mrs. Timin

Sierra ~ 4th gr.

• 1st grade •

(Timmy "1")

2nd Grade

PAINT A COLORFUL SCHOOL-THEME BORDER

Joy found inspiration for her colorful, hand-painted border and books from a piece of stationery. Begin by drawing border lines and details with pen; paint with watercolors. Crop photos; mat on solid paper trimmed with decorative scissors (Memories Forever). Freehand cut apple shape; color with watercolors. Crop individual portrait to fit apple; round corners. Finish with journaling.

Joy Carey, Visalia, California

NATE AT 8

FIRST DAY OF SCHOOL

2nd GRADE

1st Grade

COLOR BLOCK A SIMPLE SPREAD

(LEFT) A treasured postcard from a new teacher set the tone for a wonderful school year for Angie's daughter, featured on this simple color-block spread. Create border by slicing ¼" strips of solid paper; mount down sides of paper. Adhere school-theme stickers (Provo Craft) to 1½" squares; mount at corners of page. Mount postcard with clear photo corners (3L Corp.). Adhere cropped triangles to corners of one photo; mount photos. Paper tear title block; mount to page with nested eyelets (Impress Rubber Stamps; technique on page 92). Adhere sticker letters (Provo Craft). Complete page with pen line details at border, around photo and on photo corners.

Angie McGoveran, Festus, Missouri

Back 2 School

HIGHLIGHT CERTIFICATES AND REPORT CARDS

(BELOW) Including report cards and special achievement certificates helps Jennifer remember why her "good old school days" were so good! Start with alphabet paper (Me & My Big Ideas) background to provide the borders. Mat class photo and reduced color copies of school memorabilia; layer on pages. Crop die cuts (The Beary Patch) and adhere school theme stickers (Frances Meyer, Me & My Big Ideas). Cut and color title design from pattern. Cut and mat text blocks; add journaling.

Jennifer Moll, Ponca City, Oklahoma

First Day of 3rd Grade

PRESERVE LIST OF CLASSMATES' NAMES

Kerri used apple die cuts and a computer-printed list of her daughter's classmates for this easy, back-to-school page spread. Begin with patterned paper (Creative Imaginations) background. Crop, corner round, double mat photos and mount. Print and double mat captions and class list. For title, layer apple die cuts (Accu-Cut) and adhere letter stickers (Provo Craft). Mount apple below class list. Freehand cut bus shape. Accent bus with chalk, black paper stripes, black and gray circles for wheels, and pen stroke details. Silhouette-crop faces (Cock-A-Doodle Design) and layer behind windows; mount bus on page. Adhere letter stickers on bus to finish.

Kerri Brookins, Burleson, Texas

4th Grade

HIGHLIGHT PHOTO WITH PAPER FRAME

Oksanna frames her son's first day of school photo with a large apple frame and graffiti-style writing for a boyish look. Insert classroom photo into mat made with a corner slot punch (McGill); double mat on corrugated (DMD Industries) and patterned (Northern Spy) paper. Adhere to denim background paper (Frances Meyer). Freehand cut and color leaves; add to apple photo frame (Cock-a-Doodle Design); mount on page. Create title with lettering template (source unknown) and sticker letters (C-Thru Ruler). Punch small leaf (McGill); adhere to numeral "4." Finish page with graffiti journaling in thick watercolor pencils and stamped swirls (All Night Media) at bottom of page.

Oksanna Pope, Los Gatos, California

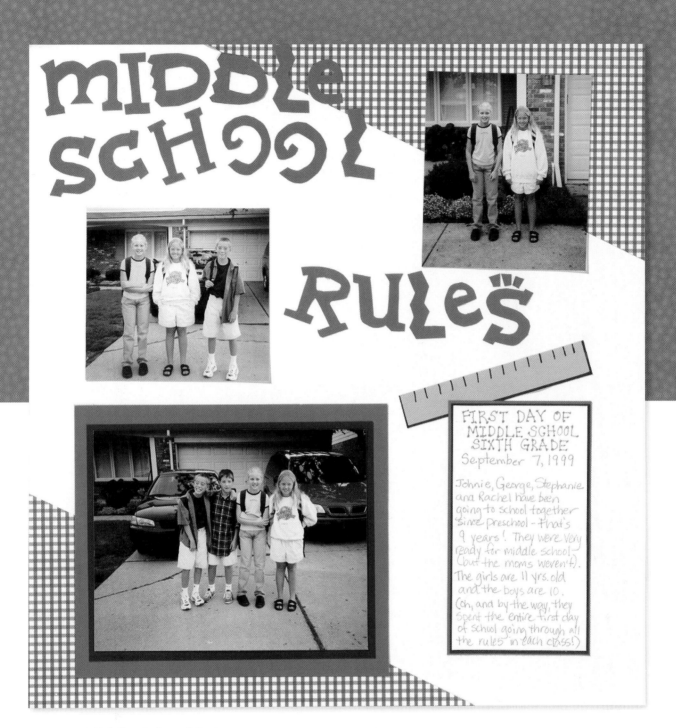

FIRST DAY OF
MIDDLE SCHOOL
SIXTH GRADE
September 7, 1999

Johnie, George, Stephanie
and Rachel have been
going to school together
since preschool - that's
9 years! They were very
ready for middle school!
(but the moms weren't).
The girls are 11 yrs. old
and the boys are 10.
(oh, and by the way, they
spent the entire first day
of school going through all
the rules in each class!)

Middle School Rules

DOCUMENT AN IMPORTANT TRANSITION

The long-awaited first day of middle school was a letdown for Karen's kids because they had to learn a whole list of their new teachers' rules and regulations. Mount patterned paper (The Paper Patch) triangles at opposite corners. Crop photos; double mat and mount. Cut title letters from template (Frances Meyer). Cut text block, double mat and add journaling. Cut rectangle for ruler; detail with black pen.

Karen Regep Glover
Grosse Pointe Woods, Michigan

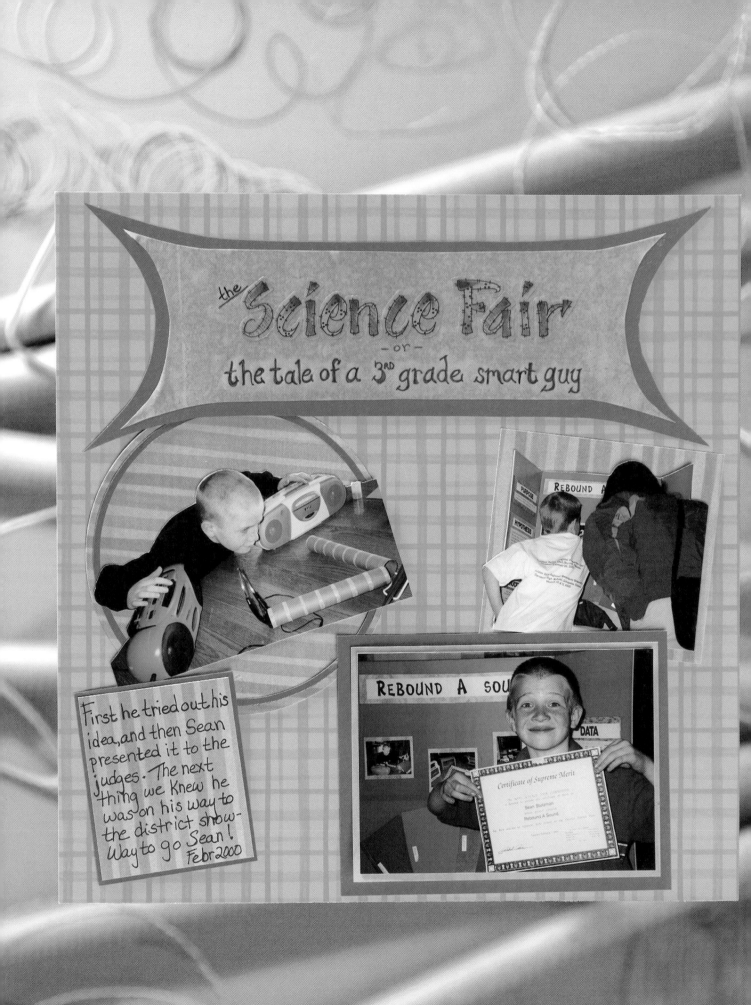

the **Science Fair**
– or –
the tale of a 3ʳᵈ grade smart guy

REBOUND A

REBOUND A SOU

DATA

Certificate of Supreme Merit

Sean Stutzman

Rebound A Sound

First he tried out his idea, and then Sean presented it to the judges. The next thing we knew he was on his way to the district show— Way to go Sean! Febr 2000

All in a Day's Work

THE SCIENCE FAIR
(SEE PAGE 125)

The most important lesson we learn in school is how to love learning. The daily lessons on math and science and language are simply the yardsticks by which we measure our success. What important and memorable yardsticks they are! Volcano models that erupt on command, that first watercolor self-portrait, a poem that brings tears to a teacher's eyes—the work of school, punctuated by the finer points of lunchroom and social etiquette, forms the structure of learning and life for children and adults. Offering their own unique mix of structure and freedom are home schooling and summer school. Yet all schoolwork produces treasures beyond compare, reminders of lessons learned, worthy of preserving and sharing with future generations.

"THEY KNOW ENOUGH WHO KNOW HOW TO LEARN."

—Henry Adams,
author and historian
(1838-1918)

MELISSA, KINDERGARTEN

Spiders

ENCOURAGE CHILD'S CREATIVITY

One of Amy's son's favorite kindergarten activities was making (and eating) edible spiders. Amy not only captured the fun in photos, but also by letting her son draw his own spider renderings on paper for the photo's background. Crop photos; round corners with decorative corner rounder punch (Marvy/Uchida). Mat on paper using decorative scissors (Frances Meyer) and add journaling to photo mats.

Amy Rognlie, Littleton, Colorado

Homework

DOCUMENT A FAVORITE ASSIGNMENT

Oksanna showed that some homework assignments can be fun and fuzzy ... like when her daughter had to take care of the "class bear." For left page, begin by layering plaid paper (Provo Craft) over solid background, leaving a ¼" border. Create photo mat using corner slot punch (All Night Media), insert photo and mat solid paper trimmed with corner rounder. Paper-piece bear (Windows of Time); detail with pen strokes. Print journal caption; trim with decorative scissors (Fiskars) and double mat. Add mini bear punches (All Night Media) on last mat. For the right page, layer plaid rectangle on background in upper right corner. Crop photo and mat; trim corners with decorative scissors. Mat two more times; trim one with corner rounder. Add punched border swirls (All Night Media) and pen strokes. Stamp bears (Duncan Enterprises); silhouette-crop and mount. Reduce and photo-copy homework page; mat and mount on page. Cut heart from template (C-Thru Ruler) and adhere; embellish with sticker letters (C-Thru Ruler), pen strokes and paw print design (All Night Media). Cut title letters using template (Provo Craft); fill in openings of letters with egg punch (EK Success); mount across bottom of both pages.

Oksanna Pope, Los Gatos, California

BEST-LOVED BOOKS ABOUT SCHOOL

Help your child fall in love with reading AND school with these fun and popular books about school!

KINDERGARTEN AND 1ST GRADE

- Arthur's Teacher Moves In *by Marc Brown*
- Froggy Goes to School *by Jonathan London*
- Hooway for Wodney Wat *by Helen Lester*
- I Spy School Days *by Jean Marzollo*
- Lilly's Purple Plastic Purse *by Kevin Henkes*
- Little Spider at Sunny Patch School *by David Kirk*
- Miss Bindergarten Gets Ready for Kindergarten *by Joseph Slate*
- Miss Nelson Is Missing *by Harry Allard*
- Officer Buckle and Gloria *by Peggy Rathman*
- Rotten Ralph Helps Out *by Jack Gantos*
- Timothy Goes to School *by Rosemary Wells*

1ST GRADE AND 2ND GRADE

- All About Stacy *by Patricia Reilly Giff*
- Amanda Pig, School Girl *by Jean Van Leeuwen*
- Junie B., First Grader (at Last) *by Barbara Park*
- Lionel at School *by Stephen Krensky*
- Marvin Redpost: Class President *by Louis Sachar*
- Meet the Barkers: Morgan and Moffat Go to School *by Tomie dePaola*
- Never Spit on Your Shoes *by Denys Cazet*
- Pinky and Rex and the School Play *by James Howe*
- Sparky and Eddie: The First Day of School *by Tony Johnston*
- The Bride of Frankenstein Doesn't Bake Cookies *by Debbie Dadey*
- Young Cam Jansen and the Lost Tooth *by David A. Adler*

3RD GRADE AND 4TH GRADE

- A Letter to Mrs. Roosevelt *by C. CoCo De Young*
- Amber Brown Goes Fourth *by Paula Danziger*
- Captain Underpants and the Perilous Plot of Professor Poopypants *by Dav Pilkney*
- Frindle *by Andrew Clements*
- Horrible Harry Goes to the Moon *by Suzy Kline*
- Judy Moody *by Megan McDonald*
- S.O.R. Losers *by Avi*
- The Best School Year Ever *by Barbara Robinson*
- The Magnificent Mummy Maker *by Elvira Woodruff*
- Thirteen Ways to Sink a Sub *by Jamie Gilson*
- Wayside School Is Falling Down *by Louis Sachar*

5TH GRADE AND 6TH GRADE

- Children of the Dust Bowl *by Jerry Stanley*
- Harry Potter series *by J.K. Rowling*
- I Was a Sixth Grade Alien *by Bruce Coville*
- Joey Pigza Swallowed the Key *by Jack Gantos*
- My Life as a Fifth Grade Comedian *by Elizabeth Levy*
- My Louisiana Sky *by Kimberly Willis Holt*
- No More Dead Dogs *by Gordon Korman*
- Outrageously Alice *by Phyllis Reynolds Naylor*
- Secret Letters from 0 to 10 *by Susie Morgenstern*
- Sixth Grade Can Really Kill You *by Barthe DeClements*
- The Austere Academy *by Lemony Snicket*
- The View From Saturday *by E.L. Konigsburg*

List courtesy of Sharon S. Ball, Multitype Consultant, North Suburban Library System, Wheeling, Illinois

GRALAND COUNTY DAY SCHOOL, 2ND GRADE

Winnie got to attend summer
school from June 4th through
June 24th, 2001 at Bustoz
Elementary School.

He learned about fosills and
dinosaurs, the Rain Forest
foliage and artifacts and
a whole bunch of other
cool stuff. He is being
taught how to learn and
the value of knowledge.

2nd Grade

Winnie, 2nd Grade

STITCH STAMPED IMAGES

Ann chose symbols to reflect the
subjects her son studied in summer
school. Begin by layering patterned
paper (source unknown) over white
paper, leaving ⅛" border. Crop photo;
mat and mount with photo corners
(Therm-O-Web). Cut title and journal
blocks, double mat and punch ⅛" circles
at bottom of one text block and top of
another. Tie together with thin jute
twine. Mount gauze (Pulsar) strip down
side of page. Stamp images (Plaid
Enterprises) with colored ink
(Clearsnap); emboss with clear embossing powder (Ranger Industries). Crop
images into rectangles and squares; stitch
borders with sewing machine or by hand.
Complete page with journaling.

Ann McElfresh, Tempe, Arizona

Dinosaur Dig

MAKE YOUR OWN PAPER-PIECING PATTERN

Marilyn caught her budding paleontologist
uncovering a hidden fossil during a class project.
Crop photos; mat and trim with decorative scissors
(Family Treasures). Add freehand cut photo corners to one photo. Create dinosaur skeleton from
photocopied and enlarged clip art (source
unknown) used for a pattern; piece together and
mount on page. Adhere sticker letters (Creative
Memories) for title. Complete with journaling.

Marilyn Garner, San Diego, California

DINOSAUR DIG

my day in grade 2

Julia Sydney Shannen

Friends

Ms. Rockwood showing us how to make book marks.

Book nook

My work

This is the lunch room. The lunch lady is making nachoes.

Me and Andrea walking to scohll.

This is my desk. picther of me and Melissa supplise. Skeeter's puppy's picther. Melissa scohll. favorite book.

I am writing in my think shop with my favorite pencil.

I am on the swings with Alena. I am at Recess.

We thought it would be fun to send a young student and scrapbooker "on assignment" to document a typical day at school. We found a willing participant in Blair, an enthusiastic second-grader at a local elementary school. To prepare for her photojournalism assignment, she made a list of all of the important photos that she planned to take—photos about things that she "wanted to remember" when she was older.

Armed with her photo list (which she later lost); a camera borrowed from her mom, Cynthia; and her teacher's permission, Blair set out one December morning to show what life is really like at her school. She began with a photo of herself and a friend trudging through the snow to school, followed by a close-up of the contents of her desk—her school supplies, photos of friends and the family dog, and a favorite reading book.

Blair also captured on film her classroom's reading nook, herself—hard at work in "the think shop," and recess fun on the swings. Some people asked Blair what she was doing, and her friends were eager to pose for pictures—some a little too eager. "My friends were crazy, and they all wanted their pictures taken," she says. "But my best friend didn't want to be in the pictures. I don't get that!"

Photos of the school lunchroom and "the lunch lady making nachos" provide great mealtime insight; while a photo of her teacher, cropped into the shape of a heart, tells a story all its own. Speaking of story, Blair's journaling tells us what her pictures could not on scrapbook pages that she created when she got her photos back from the photo lab.

Blair learned some important lessons from her assignment. "It is hard work being a photographer, and without these scrapbook pages, I think I would only remember people's faces," she says. "What will make these pages special in the future is seeing the clothes and hairstyles on the people— also my teacher's look. In 100 years, she will be 124 years old!"

We are not sure that Ms. Rockwood would like that thought, but she would probably agree with us about the grade that we gave Blair for her incredible effort to document a day at school—an "A+"! Nice job!

Blair Kacynski, Superior, Colorado

Lunch

PAPER PIECE CAFETERIA FAVORITES

Capture one of the most fun parts of a school day with paper-pieced foods! Copy and size patterns on page 121. Transfer to papers of choice, cut out and assemble.

Pamela Frye, Denver, Colorado

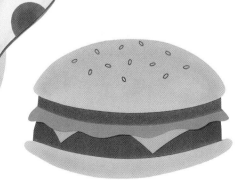

School Lunch

SERVE UP A TRAY FULL OF GOODIES

Sue relived the yummy days of lunch in the cafeteria at her grandson's school. Begin by silhouette-cropping meal tray from patterned paper (Hot Off The Press); layer on background paper. Slice out one section of the tray with a craft knife; mount photo behind cut-out area. Photocopy and size pattern for pretzels and other food items (see page 121); transfer to papers of choice and cut out. Detail with white pen. Adhere cookie stickers (Frances Meyer). Circle-cut photo and mat on patterned paper (The Paper Patch). Freehand-cut napkin from white paper, shade with pencil to create "folds." Adhere title stickers (Stickopotamus); trim and mat. Finish page with journaling.

Sue Shute, Beaver Dam, Wisconsin

Friends

ADD PLAYFULNESS TO PUNCHED SHAPES

Bold primary colors and simple use of eyelet embellishments reflect Helen's good eye for design and balance on a fun playground page. Begin by slicing ⅛" and ¼" strips of primary-colored paper. Mount ¼" strips on three sides of background paper. Crop photo and double mat. Print title and journaling; mount ⅛" strips of colored paper slightly askew around edges of text block. Add eyelets (Impress Rubber Stamps; see page 92 for technique) at paper strip intersections. Punch large flowers (Family Treasures); mount on 1¾" squares. Adhere to page and then add eyelets to center of flowers.

Helen Naylor, San Diego, California

Mad Science

CREATE THEMATIC FUN WITH FONTS

Oksanna captured the unpredictable outcome of a science experiment with a comical, paper-pieced "mad scientist" and type fonts to match. Triple mat photo using corner slot punch (McGill) for navy mat; layer on printed background paper (Provo Craft). Print titles (downloaded from Internet; source unknown) and captions on denim (Provo Craft) and colored paper; double mat caption. Cut out title letters; mat with scraps of green mulberry paper. Write small title word with black pen. Cut paper doll pieces and science "blob" monster from patterns (Scrapable Scribbles). Punch eyes with small oval and ¼" circle punches and eyebrows with moon punch (Fiskars). Cut flask from vellum paper. Complete doll science blob monster with chalk and pen stroke details.

Oksanna Pope, Los Gatos, California

Nora Loves Homework...Not!

DOCUMENT DRUDGERY WITH HUMOR

Karen loves to capture day-to-day events, even when they show one of her daughter's least favorite things to do. Note Nora's priceless expression in the lower picture. Begin by layering solid paper over patterned paper (Keeping Memories Alive), leaving ⅛" border. Crop photos and mat. For title, adhere sticker letters (C-Thru Ruler) and cut letters from template (Frances Meyer). Adhere school supplies (Stickopotamus) and student (Provo Craft) stickers to complete design.

Karen Regep Glover
Grosse Pointe Woods, Michigan

JOHNNY'S

aRt

JuNE 2000
These are Pictures
of my artwork
that I made
in 3rd grade.

Johnny's Story, 3rd grade

Throughout his third-grade year, Johnny created beautiful, priceless projects for art class. But the paper and clay weren't going to last forever, and some of the objects were too big to save. How could he preserve his artwork for the future?

With the help of his mom, Johnny took pictures of himself with his artwork and created a scrapbook spread that would keep the memories of his artwork fresh for years to come. Not only will Johnny remember his artwork, he'll remember how he looked when he made it as well. And his scrapbook page isn't just for him.

"My children and grandchildren will be able to see the things I made when I was in school," he says. Now Johnny always takes pictures of his artwork so he can remember his projects. And with his use of stickers and paper tearing, his scrapbook pages have become their own works of art to remember and cherish.

Johnny Zieske, Priest River, Idaho

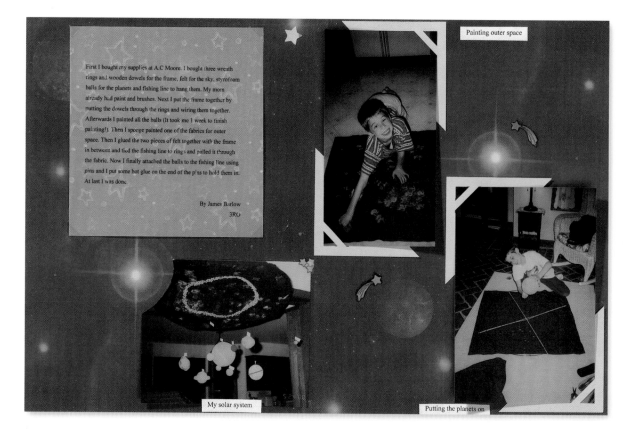

First I bought my supplies at A.C Moore. I bought three wreath rings and wooden dowels for the frame, felt for the sky, styrofoam balls for the planets and fishing line to hang them. My mom already had paint and brushes. Next I put the frame together by putting the dowels through the rings and wiring them together. Afterwards I painted all the balls (It took me 1 week to finish painting!). Then I sponge painted one of the fabrics for outer space. Then I glued the two pieces of felt together with the frame in between and tied the fishing line to rings and pulled it through the fabric. Now I finally attached the balls to the fishing line using pins and I put some hot glue on the end of the pins to hold them in. At last I was done.

By James Barlow
3RO

Painting outer space

My solar system

Putting the planets on

Putting the frame together

Painting the planets

James' Story, 3rd grade

In kindergarten, James tested into his school's "gifted program," but a little trouble with small motor skills affected his ability to write well enough to do the work required in the program. "James' mind often raced ahead of his hands, which was a real frustration for him," recalls his mom, Patty. "Scrapbooking encouraged James to journal as well as to do other small motor skill functions that helped to improve his abilities."

In third grade, James put his mastered skills to the test for an assignment in Mrs. Roche's class: He designed and built a solar system and documented his project in a scrapbook. His celestial success includes photos that show every step of the project. And his grade? "100% or an 'A'," says James.

"I liked making it but not doing the oral presentation," he says. "And everyone loved it! I was the only one who used a scrapbook or even used pictures." Years from now, James will likely remember that he got an awesome grade on the project, but without the scrapbook, "I don't think I'd remember how I made the solar system," he says.

James still scrapbooks about his dad, his mom, his activities and his cat. James' advice to other students about scrapbooking class projects? "Try it; it's cool. And you just might get a really good grade!"

James William Barlow III, Downingtown, Pennsylvania

In fifth grade, Gary had to visit a California mission and then build a replica, make a videotape or write a report about the mission and the trip. "My mom was scrapbooking, and I thought it might be more fun and easier than the other choices," says Gary.

"I liked visiting the San Juan Capistrano Mission and taking the photographs," he continues. "I liked matching the colors to the page and drawing the swallows. I like to draw and this gave me a chance to include my drawings in the project."

Gary had never worked on a scrapbook before, and he worked on the project at a scrapbook workshop he attended with his mom, Elisa. "My teacher really liked the album, and Mom shows the book to all her scrapping friends," Gary says.

In his opinion, "journaling helps keep track of what is going on at the time, where you are, and when it is. It helps you remember things later," says Gary. "I didn't think I'd like that part (the journaling), but I kept wanting to add things I had forgotten, so I'd just write them on the page."

Since his school project, Gary has created enough scrapbook pages to fill an album. His pages feature his cats, the zoo, bowling, his own lettering and his drawings. He attends a scrapbook workshop monthly. "Most of the time I am the youngest person there and almost always the only guy," he says with a smile.

"Without my album, I probably wouldn't remember much about the trip," says Gary. "Maybe the Mission won't be here 100 years from now and people will be able to see what it was like and learn about it from my album."

The final touch on Gary's album? A tiny photo of him cleverly tucked behind an old mission door on the very last page. It is the perfect ending.

Gary Purnell, Camarillo, California

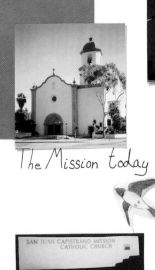

The Mission today

Mission San Juan Capistrano was founded twice. The first time was in 1775 by Father Lauseun and the second time was in 1776 by Father Serra. Father Serra dug up the bells that Father Lauseun had buried before and hung them from a tree.

SAN JUAN CAPISTRANO MISSION CATHOLIC CHURCH

Mission San Juan Capistrano

by Gary S. Purnell
1999

Much of the memorabilia that finds its way home during the grade school years is a child's artwork. Like many parents, the art covers the refrigerator, or like Theresa's, it is featured on a "wall of fame" at home. One such piece of art is a playground drawing that her daughter, Audrey, created for a contest.

Audrey was a finalist in a "Draw Your Dream Playground" contest sponsored by the Elizabethtown Playground Committee. "I learned that I could let my imagination run free with ideas of things that I'd really like to have on my own dream playground," Audrey says. "Now I can remember the contest every time I look at the page Mom did!"

Construction on the playground began last spring. "It was a special moment in Audrey's life, and hopefully she can reflect on it with her children or grandchildren and they can go visit the real playground together!" says Theresa.

Theresa Smith, Elizabethtown, Kentucky

Brice's Winning Streak

RECORD SCHOLASTIC ACCOMPLISHMENTS

Donna was inspired by a timeline feature in a previous issue of *Memory Makers* magazine to create a layout of her daughter's academic triumphs. Begin by slicing ¼" strips of paper; mount vertically to create "columns" and show direction on patterned paper (Keeping Memories Alive) background. Crop photos; trim with corner rounder and mat on pat-terned paper (source unknown). Print journaling; crop to size and mat on solid paper. Adhere sticker letters (Creative Memories) for title and category headings on white paper; trim to size and mat. Adhere school-theme stickers (Creative Memories, Frances Meyer).

Donna Fenton, Williamstown, West Virginia

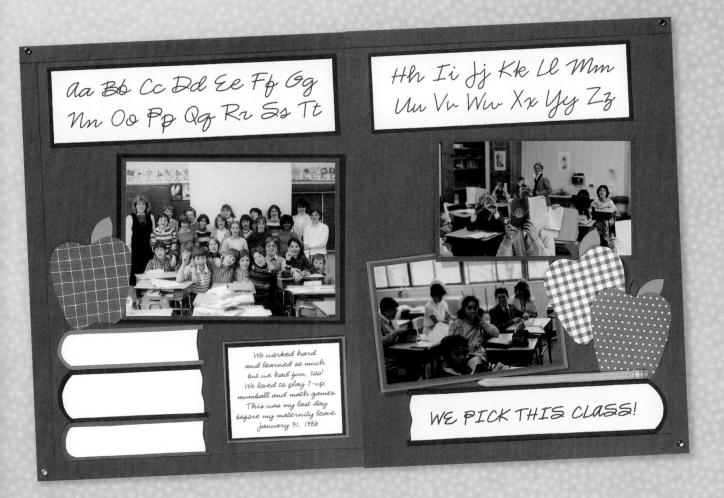

We Pick This Class!

PAPER PIECE SCHOOL-THEME SYMBOLS

Debbie records fond memories of teaching with timeless school symbols. Begin by slicing six ½" wide strips; mount over solid background paper at edges. Adhere small fasteners (HyGlo/American Pin) at outside page corners. Crop photos; single and double mat. Copy and size book and apple patterns (see page 120). Cut pattern pieces from solid and patterned papers (Doodlebug Design, Frances Meyer, Making Memories); piece together and layer on page as shown. Adhere pencil sticker (Me & My Big Ideas) on white cardstock; silhouette and mat with self-adhesive foam spacers. Print script font title, journaling and alphabet; cut to size and mat before mounting on page.

Idea and Patterns Chris Peterson
Lakewood, Colorado

Photos and Layout Debby Schuh, The Memory Bee
Clarence, New York

Punch-n-Stitch

It is easy to create homespun appeal on a scrapbook page by using a variety of stitches, such as a simple running straight stitch, a cross stitch or an overcast stitch, shown on the page below. Experiment with stitches like the blanket stitch, chain stitch, or daisy stitch for completely different effects. You don't have to be a needlepoint enthusiast to skillfully add this look to your scrapbook pages. Your local library or the Internet (search words: needlepoint stitches) can provide great illustrations of basic to complex stitches.

School

STITCH A PUNCHED PAGE

Alison's simple stitching is a charming complement to her scrapbook page that features classroom photos. Although Alison's page is a 12 x 12" scrapbook page, you can easily use this technique on any size page. To create your own similar look, begin with a cardstock background in the color of your choice. Crop and mat photos; adhere to page. Cut white mats from cardstock for journaling block and for stitching. Then follow the steps below to create the page. Finish with journaling.

Alison Beachem, San Diego, California

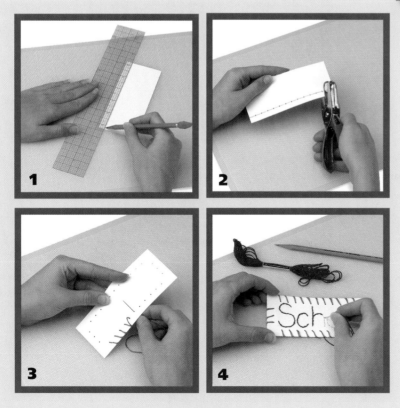

1 *To begin, use a ruler and a pencil to draw "dots" that will serve as punch guidelines at ½" intervals around the page's edge and around pre-cut mats (Figure 1).*

2 *Use a ¹⁄₁₆" round hand punch to punch dots (Figure 2), creating the "holes" used for stitching.*

3 *Thread embroidery floss of choice into a sewing needle and stitch around the page's edges and the mat edges (Figure 3); tie off ends on back of page and mats.*

4 *To create lettering on mats, use a pencil to draw dots to form letters. Pierce the dots with a sewing needle to create holes for stitching. Stitch letters using a simple running stitch (Figure 4). If desired, stitch edges of apple die cuts, as shown; adhere to mat. Assemble all stitched mats and mount in place on page.*

Crafty Crayons

PUNCH AND PIECE A CRAYON BORDER

Alexandra's colorful punch art border is a perfect accent for scrapbook pages that display children's art and art class photos. Begin with a 2" strip of black paper for border background. Punch white 1¹¹⁄₁₆" deco squares (Family Treasures); adhere to background. Punch picket borders (Emagination Crafts) from primary-colored papers; cut pickets in half to form "crayons." Add freehand-cut rectangles of same-color shades of primary colors atop crayons to create "paper wrap." Assemble four crayons atop each white square with tips meeting in center as shown.

Alexandra Bleicher, Chilliwack, British Columbia, Canada

Notebooks

PUNCH SCHOOL SUBJECTS THEME BOOKS

Class curriculum scrapbook pages get off to a quick-and-easy start with Alexandra's simple punched border of "notebooks." Start with a 1⅞" strip of red paper matted with a 1½" strip of black paper for background. For each notebook, punch two ¾" squares (The Punch Bunch) from colored paper and one from white paper. Assemble notebook "pages" as shown; adhere to border strip. Accent pages with white halved ½" squares (The Punch Bunch); add subject title with pen.

Alexandra Bleicher, Chilliwack, British Columbia, Canada

Loving Hands

PUNCH A HANDPRINT BORDER

Alison's punched handprint border is a nice complement to scrapbook pages featuring a child's handprint or other artwork. First, create "mats" by layering punched 1⁹⁄₁₆" and 1¼" squares (Family Treasures); assemble and adhere on page in an offset manner as shown. Top squares with punched hands (EK Success) accented with mini hearts (Fiskars).

Alison Beachem, San Diego, California

Home Schooling

Basketball practice, math and English class, social studies and art. Just another busy day at school, except that in this school classes take place at the kitchen table, recess is in the backyard and the ballgames are all played at the local recreation center. With everything happening under their own roofs, home-schooling families certainly have no shortage of material for their scrapbooks. Read on for scrapbooking stories from home schoolers.

Johnna's Story

While students in traditional schools are slide shows of the Renaissance painters, Johnna Pierson and her children are visiting the museums of Paris. And while the kids back home are studying the history of Latin America, Johnna's family is standing at the base of pyramids in Mexico.

As a scrapbooking veteran Johnna knew there was no better way to document their traveling classroom than to bring scrapbooking into school. "It's a great way to remember where we've been and whom we have met," she says. Johnna has everyone carry his or her own camera, take pictures and make scrapbook pages of family field trips.

Not only does scrapbooking provide a format for preserving great memories, it has also helped with virtually every aspect of schoolwork, Johnna says. She sees improvements in handwriting and a better understanding of logic. "It has helped with learning to 'see' things that would make a good page," she says.

And with her husband's job taking the family someplace new every ten months, Johnna has been able to incorporate some amazing sights into her daily lesson plan. For Johnna, home schooling doesn't always mean school "at home." Between field trips to the pyramids of Mexico, the Eiffel Tower in Paris and all the monuments in Washington, D.C., it's obvious that Johnna doesn't take the "home" part of home schooling too literally.

Johnna Pierson, Greenville, South Carolina

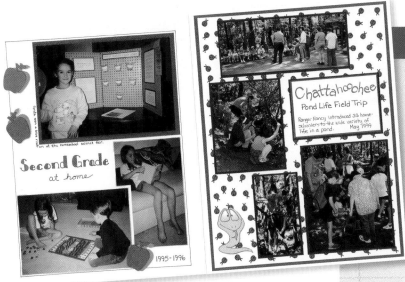

Second Grade
at home

1995-1996

Chattahoochee
Pond Life Field Trip

Ranger Nancy introduced 33 homeschoolers to the wide variety of
life in a pond. May 1999

Adrian's Story

Choosing to home school your children can provide your family with certain freedoms not available to families using traditional schools. Your children are able to learn at a pace best suited for them; your family can travel any time of the year. And you can ensure that your children are getting the attention they deserve and need. But there are some things home schoolers don't get that children in regular classrooms do—yearbooks, class pictures and other mementos. Adrian found a simple and creative solution to that problem. "I create a page for each grade for their own albums, documenting some of the special, and ordinary, activities they do in school," she says. Throughout the year she takes pictures of everything from the days spent studying at the kitchen table to the days spent out on field trips. "My children will never forget the autumn we went on a Caribbean cruise," she says. "They had home school on the pool deck a few mornings, in their bathing suits, with a view over the ocean."

When it comes to other forms of memorabilia, Adrian believes that the occasional "Student of the Week" or "Best Improved Handwriting" goes a long way. However, she prefers her scrapbooks to contain mainly photos and keeps the other memorabilia in personal journals. "It's the student's own work that holds meaning in years to come," she says.

Adrian Noren, Marietta, Georgia

Susan's Story

When Susan began home schooling 13 years ago, she knew she would be facing an uphill battle to convince others that she was doing the right thing. "I also wanted to prove to people that I don't sit around eating bonbons and watching soap operas while my kids read books," she says. Susan's need to prove herself inspired her to begin keeping what she calls a "school portfolio," or scrapbook, for each of her four children. In the scrapbooks, she includes samples of their schoolwork as well as photos from activities and field trips that show that her children really were having school. But Susan's style of "record-keeping" did more than just convince her friends of the legitimacy of home schooling. They liked the idea of keeping samples and memorabilia so much that some of them began creating their own scrapbooks.

Today, with the pressure to prove herself long gone, Susan is able to use scrapbooking as a way to make school more fun. Her children work on their own scrapbooks in art class—cutting, arranging and choosing their photos—which allows them to explore and express their creativity. And best of all, Susan is able to look at these books and recall how much fun they've had and how much her children have grown.

"I'm glad that I felt pressured to prove myself to others because now I have great school scrapbooks to look through," she says.

Susan Seydel, Bonita, California

Home Schoolers: Busy as Bees!

Our new Homeschool support group, Midcoast Christian Homeschoolers, just started this semester. Some of the kids who are also in AWANA needed to visit an historic place in their books. So, we decided to visit the Maine State Museum in Augusta. Four families met there and toured the whole place. We Mom's decided that we would like to take our own trip there, just so we could take the time to read all the info at our own pace!

Later in the semester we had a spelling Bee. Dawn got behind that and ran it wonderfully for us. She gathered up grade level spelling lists to study. On that day we lined the kids all up according to grade level and tested them from their own lists. All of the kids did very well. In the end, Katherine Nadeau, one of our second graders, proved herself most proficient at her list! She was awarded a ribbon donated to us by the shop that we bought the participation awards from. I think we will do this event again!

Diane's Story

Whenever anyone questions Diane's decision to home school her children, she has one perfect response: her scrapbook. "When it comes to convincing those who are unsure about the fact that we home school, a viewing of the scrapbook usually will open eyes and minds," Diane says.

The days of the isolated home schooler are long gone, and Diane is more than happy to help shatter that image. Her scrapbooks of spelling bees and field trips to museums and farms are proof enough that her children aren't lacking in any socialization or public recognition. "Home-school families take such pains to be sure that their children have outside interaction in the 'real world' that we need a place to stash those achievement certificates," she says. With awards earned through sports, scouting, church, reading and countless other activities, Diane's children have received as much as, or even more, recognition than many students in public school.

But Diane doesn't believe that all of her children's accomplishments need to be recognized with assemblies and award ceremonies. "The most valuable recognition comes when extended family and friends see their scrapbooked school memories and applaud them with hugs and words of encouragement!" Diane says. "At times like those, family members often launch into their own memories of school days." That's when her children learn more about their family heritage—something that they could never learn in a traditional classroom. "I wouldn't give that up for all the recognition assemblies in the world!" she says.

Diane Simmler, Bath, Maine

Amy's Story

With scrapbooking, Amy is able to provide the home-school review board with more colorful records of her children's schoolwork than just a written list of what they've studied. "It's one thing to show our portfolio with the sentence 'We cooked an Egyptian meal for Grandma and Grandpa,' and quite another to take them through our unit study in pictures!" she says. And with many of their lessons being hands-on projects, Amy says she would rather not drag all of the models, costumes and meals they make to the review office. But the scrapbooks aren't just for the review board.

Amy uses them to bring her family closer together. "It's a nice way for the kids to sit down with aunts and uncles and grandparents and go over what they've done." The books also add fun to the classroom. "I tend to be very artistic, so we bring lots of little scrapbooking concepts into class. If I can hand them something that's creative to do, the learning will sink in," Amy says. But beyond helping to educate her children, Amy says there's another, even greater benefit to the time she and her kids spend scrap-booking. "I'm bonding with the most important people in my life," she says.

Amy Moxley, Mount Airy, Maryland

Activities &
Special Events

"HOW DOTH THE LITTLE BUSY BEE

IMPROVE EACH SHINING HOUR,

AND GATHER HONEY ALL THE DAY

FROM EVERY OPENING FLOWER!"

—*Isaac Watts, Author (1674-1748)*

If schoolwork is the pencil sketch, then activities and special events are the colors that complete the masterpiece of education. In sports, children learn the value—and the challenges—of teamwork. On stage, they harness the butterflies within to soar aloft. During field trips, kids step through Alice's looking glass to touch new worlds. Celebrations set the hearts of children free. With awards and ceremonies, children learn to honor not just achievement but also the quest for achievement itself. The more a child does, the more photos and memorabilia there are to treasure and preserve in scrapbooks. Be sure to save sports ribbons, citizenship certificates and copies of recited poems. Each reveals a golden moment worth remembering.

ANNA, 5TH GRADE

LADY STORM
(SEE PAGE 125)

Sports

Whether children participate in a team or an individual sport, playing sports teaches children valuable lessons in perseverance, discipline and integrity. Preserve these memories with photos of the special people involved and memorabilia that captures the excitement of a season. Win or lose, children's sports memories are an important part of the grade school experience.

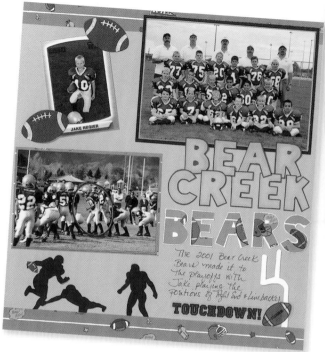

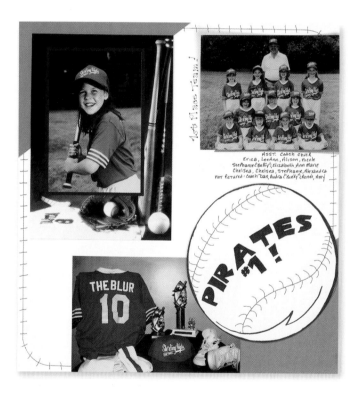

Pirates #1!

PHOTOGRAPH SPORTS MEMORABILIA

Tammy's daughter loves to play a variety of sports, so at the end of every season, Tammy makes sure she photographs the team uniform amongst season-winning memorabilia. Mount colored triangles in two colors. Crop photos; mount one on colored triangle. Circle-cut large baseball. Add red "stitching" to ball and around page with pen. Complete page with team name on ball and journaling under photo. See page 125 for tips on photographing memorabilia.

Tammy Meerschaert, Sterling Heights, Michigan

Bear Creek Bears

HIGHLIGHT STAR PLAYER ON THE FIELD

MaryJo's son enjoyed a winning season and superstar status on a page highlighting his achievements. Begin by slicing ⅞" strips of patterned paper (Frances Meyer); mount at upper and lower edges of page. Add pen stroke details to football die cut (Creative Memories); tuck behind lower border as shown. Crop photos; double mat on solid and patterned papers (Frances Meyer). Crop an oval into one photo to highlight player; double mat and adhere over original photo with self-adhesive foam spacers. Mount photo player card; layer die-cut footballs (Creative Memories) with pen stroke details in white ink. Cut title letters using template (Scrap Pagerz) from solid and patterned papers. Mat and silhouette; add dimension with chalk around the edges. Complete with journaling and football stickers (Creative Memories).

Design Kelly Angard, Highlands Ranch, Colorado

Photos MaryJo Regier, Littleton, Colorado

Sports Theme Album

PRESERVE THE SEASON'S HIGHLIGHTS

Long after the equipment is put away and the blood, sweat and tears have dried, the memories remain in Cathy's sports albums—all four of them!

Because she has so many games to record, Cathy separates the seasons by repeating the same design elements—in this case, stamped and silhouette-cropped stars, computer-printed journaling and the same paper colors—within each particular sports season.

Cathy's albums also include newspaper clippings, great action shots, still photos, even photos of the scoreboard. Lest a memory be forgotten, her extensive journaling includes names of coaches and players, inspirational sports-related sayings, season stats and highlights, trivia about the team, and quotes about the coaches and the season offered by individual players. One thing is certain: Win or lose, sports albums score!

Cathy Gray, Fayetteville, Tennessee

2001
11-12 Year old Little League Health Care Resources Team

Coaches: Dale Moran, Philip Shelton Bob Gray
Players: Ryan Holmes, Bruce Beddingfield, Matt Moran, Clint Snoddy, Casey Beddingfield, Chris Harris, Eric Berngruber, Rob Gray, Zerian Mastin, Chris Shelton, Chris Mitchell, Jeremiah Thomas

Did You know?
- Hot Dogs at the concession stand sell for $1.00
- Cokes for $1.00
- Nachos and cheese- $1.25
- An Easton Bat- 189.00
- A uniform- $50.00
- A glove $60.00- 100.00
- Cleats $60.00
  2001

How to identify a real fan?
- hears "Please return all foul balls to the concession stand" in his dreams
- sets up a chair but never sits in it because they're too nervous
- has a passion for the game
- plans summer vacations around baseball games
- goes to the ballpark early and stays late to watch the other teams play
- is know to say "just one more out boys" about 20 times a game
- Sunflower seeds are his favorite snack
- Can't sleep after a close game
- Over analyzes every game
- Starts 50% of his sentences with "If we just had _____ (fill in blank)

Little League- A Nervous Break Down one inning at a time.

My favorite game- who can possibly forget this one? 1 to 1 in the seventh inning. Rob and Chris pitched fantastic. No errors in the field. Eric came in and pitched like a man. We lost, but I was so proud of the boys. They played their hearts out.

Indian Heights Basketball

SHOW CONTINUITY ON A TWO-PAGE LAYOUT

Heather searched for a way to display a full season of basketball photos while maintaining a cohesive two-page design. To create the nine-photo layout on the left, she used an octagon template and arranged photos in a circle. Center large photo; fill white spaces with small solid and patterned (Hot Off The Press) paper triangles. Crop and double mat photos on righthand page with same papers. Create border down side of page with triangles in same size and papers as opposite page; adhere to page leaving white space between triangles. Complete page with border lines on both pages and journaling with calligraphy pen.

Heather McWhorter, Kokomo, Indiana

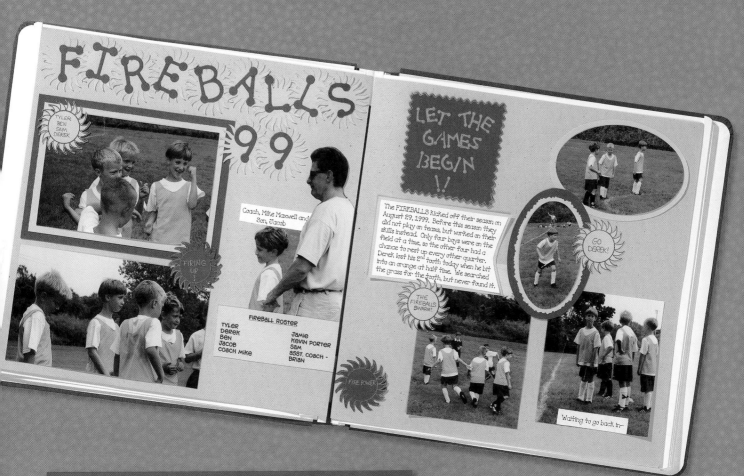

Chris' Story, 3rd grade

School activities pass so quickly; it can be hard to remember all the details. Chris recorded his memories of a charity event by scrapbooking about it.

"What I like most about scrapbooking is that you get to keep the memories more accurately than when you just have pictures," he says. Years later, he'll remember what happened and who was there.

"It will show me some of my childhood friends and the things I liked to do. And I'll be able to share it with other people," he says.

Scrapbooking has taught him a valuable lesson. "If you want to preserve memories well, think about it and do not just throw something together or not even do it at all," he says.

Chris Tardie, Berlin, Vermont

Fireballs 99

ADD PUNCH TO PAGE TITLE

Joellyn captures the enthusiasm of her son's first soccer team experience. Begin by cropping photos into ovals and squares. Single and double mat a few; trim one mat with decorative scissors. Punch jumbo suns (Family Treasures); layer across top of page. Mount die-cut title letters (Accu-Cut) over sunbursts. Stamp sun design (Stampabilities) on punched suns; layer on page for photo caption blocks. Crop printed journaling and mat and mount on page. Draw subtitle letters with template (source unknown); cut to size and trim with decorative scissors.

Joellyn Borke Johnston, Des Moines, Iowa

Lone Star Cyclones

CREATE A "FLIP-UP" MINI ALBUM

Heather found a way to display many photos by integrating a "flip-up" mini album on her pages. Begin by cropping photos for flip-up layers to 4 x 4½"; slip into clear photo sleeves (DMD Industries). Layer on background patterned paper (NRN Designs) as shown; adhere with wide sticker strips (Mrs. Grossman's) cut to size. Crop side photos; mat one and adhere stickers at corners (It Takes Two). Mount other photo behind decorative paper frame (My Mind's Eye). Cut 2" strip of patterned paper (Sandylion) for title block. Layer ¼" paper strip over patterned paper. Cut title letters using template (EK Success); mat and silhouette. Mount star fasteners (HyGlo/American Pin) on letters. Complete page by printing journaling; cut to size and mat.

Heather Shepherd, Sanger, California

Angelica

DESIGN A TEAM JERSEY

After attending a goal-making soccer game, Suzy knew her niece deserved to be highlighted in her scrapbook! Begin by mounting a solid, team-colored triangle in the corner. Copy and enlarge "jersey" pattern (see page 120); detail with hand-cut numbers and sticker letters (Making Memories). Crop photos and round photos' corners. Mount soccer ball die cut (Ellison); detail with pens and mat on cardstock. Cut out text block, mat and journal.

Suzy Quimbaya, Maumee, Ohio

Performances

In the center-stage spotlight, children learn how to channel their jitters into something wonderful—a sparkling performance that is a gift to the audience. Tuck away scripts and programs from plays and sheet music from recitals for display in your scrapbooks.

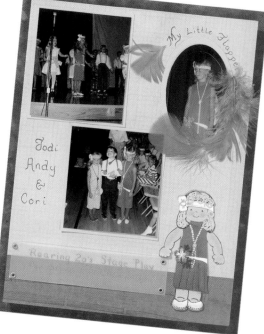

My Little Flapper
SAVE TIDBITS OF COSTUME

Cheryl sets the stage with feathers saved from a costume and a paper doll dressed to match. Begin with patterned paper background (Fiskars). Slice a 2" strip of solid brown paper; stamp wood print (Clearsnap) design to resemble stage floor. Crop photos and mat. Stamp doll parts (Joyful Hearts Stamps); silhouette, assemble, and add details to match photo. Punch mini swirls (All Night Media) for hair; mini oak leaf and mini flower (EK Success) for dress; and freehand cut bow for hair. Add pen and chalk details. Add feathers around photo. Journal on vellum; mount to page with colored eyelets (HyGlo/American Pin).

Cheryl Delavan, Cherry Valley, Illinois

Friends
SHOWCASE A SPECIAL PERFORMANCE

Lisa's daughter felt like the star of the show in a new dress at her kindergarten musical show. Begin by layering patterned paper (Design Originals) over solid, leaving ¼" border. Crop photos and reduced, photocopied musical program; single and double mat. Mount treble clef die cuts (Ellison).

Lisa Langhans, Lake Villa, Illinois

California Hoedown

FRAME PHOTOS WITH ROPE DESIGN

Jeanne's son got "roped" into square dancing at his school's country hoedown. Begin by cropping photos into ovals; mount on page. Freehand draw rope design to "lasso" photos. Add "caller" clip art (source unknown); color with pencils. Write title, journaling and dot details with pens. Adhere musical note stickers (Mrs. Grossman's).

Jeanne Ciolli, Dove Canyon, California

School Program

PHOTOCOPY PROGRAMS OF PLAYS

Pat enjoyed creating her punch-art piggies to accent photocopies of her granddaughter's school play. Crop photos and mat. Reduce and photocopy program; mat on solid paper. Silhouette-crop and mat page topper (Cock-a-Doodle Design) for title. Create punch-art piggies with 1¼" and ⅝" circle, small swirl, mini heart, small bow for feet, mini diamond and dot for eyes and large maple leaf (all Family Treasures), trimmed for ears. Freehand cut and slice colored paper for sticks, straw and bricks. Circle-cut text block and mat. Punch and assemble daisies (Family Treasures); adhere. Freehand cut arrow and add journaling to finish the page.

Pat Asher, Camarillo, California

Musical Celebration

LAYER A MUSICAL MONTAGE

(ABOVE) Sarah documents a lovely afternoon picnic and end-of-the-year musical event put on by the children at her daughter's school. With her photo montage, she is able to fit a lot of photos onto each page. Begin by cropping photos, overlaying them as you go to fit within the frame of the patterned paper (Design Originals). When you are pleased with the arrangement of the photos, mount in place with adhesive.

Sarah McKenna, Gloucestershire, England

The Lion King

COORDINATE THEME WITH PATTERNED PAPERS

(BELOW) Patti shows her daughter is star of the show by combining wild animal prints and stickers with photos of an exciting stage production. Crop photos; mat photos on solid and animal print patterned papers (Frances Meyer, The Paper Patch). Crop and place photos behind large paw print die cut (Ellison). Adhere large animal stickers (Mrs. Grossman's), incorporating them to look as if they are holding photos. Adhere title sticker letters (Making Memories); outline with black pen.

Patti Holland, San Jose, California

Clubs & Activities

From merit badges and honor ribbons to service projects and after-school meetings—as your children become joiners, their efforts build a pool of memories and mementos. Clubs and activities provide a venue for individual and group achievement as children learn that the power of "we" is far greater than the power of "me."

Oceanography Club

PAPER TEAR A "SEA-NIC" ADVENTURE

Maggie incorporated photos from a weekend field trip into a paper-torn sea scene. Freehand tear paper pieces for sun, boat, whale and land. Crop and silhouette photos; layer among paper torn scene. Adhere sea life stickers (Mrs. Grossman's, Stickopotamus). Write title, journaling and photo captions; accent with decorative pen strokes, swirls and details.

Maggie Bilash, Mesa, Arizona

4-H

PRESERVE A NEWSPAPER CLIPPING

Heather documented her daughter's showmanship experience at the county fair by including a newspaper photo encased in an acid-free memorabilia envelope (Creative Memories). Create the colorful border by drawing the thick and thin straight lines first. Use decorative ruler (Creative Memories) to draw the ribbon effect; shade with pen. Freehand draw four-leaf clover in corner. Adhere colored paper triangles in opposite corners; mount 4-H letters (Creative Memories). Crop photos and round corners. Complete page with journaling and cat and rabbit punches (Nankong).

Heather McWhorter, Kokomo, Indiana

Troop 265
DRESS UP A BACKGROUND

As a Brownie Scout troop leader, Lorie values the importance of celebrating girls and their achievements. Freehand cut vest for background. Punch medium and small circles for "buttons" and "pins"; add flower and star stickers (Creative Memories, Stickopotamus). Cut triangles and mat to resemble patches and adhere stickers (Creative Memories, Mrs. Grossman's). Adhere black stickers (Provo Craft) for title. Adhere white sticker letters (Creative Memories) for troop identification; cut to size and mount. Crop photos; mount on page. Complete page with journaling.

Lorie Graham, Lexington, South Carolina

Chess
CRAFT OVERSIZED GAME PIECES

Oksanna's son takes on a new challenge by joining his school's chess club. Layer patterned paper (Provo Craft) over solid paper for the background. Freehand cut chess piece from solid paper. Crop photos; mat one and mount all on page. Cut title letters using template (C-Thru Ruler); add pen stroke details. Stamp ornamental design (All Night Media) and complete with pen stroke detail around photo.

Oksanna Pope, Los Gatos, California

Girl Scout Cookie Time
STACK A PILE OF COOKIE BOXES

When Angela's daughter sold almost 300 boxes of Girl Scout cookies, her living room turned into a cookie warehouse with stacks of boxes all around. Crop panoramic photo and mat. Freehand cut cookie boxes from colored cardstock; detail with pens. Write creative title letters with pens on vellum trimmed with decorative scissors; double mat. Punch 1" circles from brown paper for cookies; detail with pen. Complete page with matted journaling.

Angela Newton, Pewee Valley, Kentucky

Junior Girl Scout Rachel
PRESERVE UNIFORM WITH PAPER DOLL

Even without any photos, Karen found a way to capture her daughter's year in junior Girl Scouts with a paper doll and a photocopy of a vest. Begin by layering two colors of cardstock over background paper, leaving 1/8" border at each layer. Lightly pencil journaling border with a decorative ruler (Creative Memories). Journal with pen and erase pencil lines when ink is dry. Create paper doll (Stamping Station); add vest details with metallic stickers (Hambly Studios), punched mini circles and pen stroke details. Reduce and color photocopy front and back of vest to show patches earned; silhouette-crop photocopies and layer on page. Create "wood" frame for text block by slicing strips of patterned paper (Hot Off The Press) trimmed at the ends with decorative scissors. Mount thin twine tied into a bow and add journaling to complete.

Karen Regep Glover
Grosse Pointe Woods, Michigan

Crossing Over
TIE UP A SCOUTING ACHIEVEMENT

Gail's son "crossed over" to a new level in the Cub Scouts with countless hours of dedication and determination. Begin by cropping triangles; use fleur-de-lis corner punch (All Night Media) to accent corners before mounting at page corners. Crop photos and double mat on solid paper. Punch fleurs-de-lis at corners of second mat; mount on page. Photocopy and size pattern for neckerchief (see page 120). Cut from two colors of solid paper and assemble. Create lion cub pin from jumbo sunburst, 1" circle and small oval (Family Treasures) punches. Layer and detail with pens. Complete page with title sticker letters (Creative Memories) and add journaling.

Gail Birkhead, Tyngsboro, Massachusetts

Scouting
COMBINE PAPER SIZES

Kym found a way to integrate the perfect 8½ x 11" patterned paper for her son's scouting photos on a 12 x 12" page. Layer patterned paper (Bo-Bunny Press) over solid background paper. Crop photos; triple mat. Cut text block; triple mat. Cut 1⅝ x 10⅜" strip for title block; double mat. Freehand cut title letters; mount on title block.

Kym Gould, Greensboro, North Carolina

Bear Graduation
ADD A REALISTIC ELEMENT WITH COLOR COPIES

Jeanne added a realistic element to a Cub Scout graduation scene by nestling reduced copies of Boy Scout periodicals into the hands of paper dolls. Begin with patterned paper (Sonburn) background. Crop photos and round corners. Mat on cardstock trimmed with decorative corner and fleur-de-lis punches (Family Treasures). Mat again on cardstock; trim to size of first mat and add ¼" paper strips. Stamp title letters (Close To My Heart) on 1" squares; shade with colored pencils and mat. Stamp paper dolls (Joyful Heart Stamps);

St. Matthew's Catholic School
SHOW OFF CLUB EMBLEM

Donna created a clean and classic layout for her favorite Cub Scout portraits. Double layer tan speckled cardstock (Bazzill) over orange and blue cardstock, leaving ¼" border at each layer. Crop photos and double

mat. Create large fleur-de-lis from pattern (Windows of Time) to mimic emblem ; mat on solid paper. For title block, mat rectangle and layer over matted square. Add title text and pen stroke stitching to finish.

Donna Commons, Jacksonville, Florida

silhouette-crop and assemble. Add reduced, color-copied magazine covers; layer under boys' hands. Freehand draw flags; embellish with star and fleur-de-lis punches and pens. Slice ¼" strips and punch ⅛" circles from gold and silver metallic cardstock (Paper Cuts) for flagpoles. Complete page with paper caps (Ellison); cut front panel in complementary color and add Boy Scout stickers (Boy Scouts of America).

Jeanne Ciolli, Dove Canyon, California

Field Trips

On field trips kids get a chance to step outside of their normal routine and discover new worlds. The warm, yeasty smell of the bakery; the sounds of all the farm animals; the bustle of the factory all yield wonderful memories that can be captured with journaling and photos.

January 26, 2001

Frozen Field Trip

PAPER PIECE FAVORITE PART OF A FIELD TRIP

A little winter weather didn't spoil the fun of Lori's son's kindergarten field trip. Begin by layering patterned paper (Making Memories) over solid paper, leaving ¼" border. Paper piece school buses with pattern (Windows of Time); detail with pen. Add freehand paper-pieced bus driver and photo on back of bus. Crop photos; single and double mat.

Layer photos, buses and white paper-torn strips for "snow" on page. Print poem; trim and mat. Add small photo silhouette and freehand cut arrows to highlight child. Freehand draw title letters on 1⁵⁄₁₆" squares and large rectangle. Outline title; color with pencils and mat.

Lori Bowders, Waynesboro, Pennsylvania

Field Trip

ADD PIZAZZ WITH CORNER PUNCH DETAILS

There's no better school day for a student than one that includes a field trip, no matter where the destination. Oksanna documents her son's trip to a research center with bold colors and simple details. Start with patterned paper (The Robin's Nest Press) background. Crop photos into shapes. Single and double mat photos on solid paper; detail two mats with decorative corner slot punches (Fiskars). Create title letters with template (Provo Craft) in two colors and layer to create shadow effect; fill in holes in letters with swirl punch (All Night Media). Complete page with punched stars (Emagination Crafts) and journaling.

Oksanna Pope, Los Gatos, California

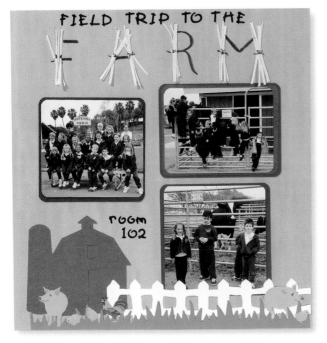

Field Trip to the Farm

ADD DIMENSION WITH CREATIVE LETTERING

Jacquie looked no further than her photos for inspiration when designing and selecting colors for her son's field trip page. Begin by cropping photos; round corners. Single and double mat. Layer over patterned paper (Sandylion). Craft farm scene at bottom of page with die cut barn (Ellison), fence (Stamping Station) and grass (Accu-Cut). Adhere farm animal stickers (Mrs. Grossman's). Slice thin strips of ivory cardstock; overlap and adhere together to form parts of letters. Complete letters with pen. Adhere sticker letters (Provo Craft) for title and date.

Jacquie Lomax, Long Beach, California

Our Field Trip to Chief Mountain

CRAFT SOME CLASSROOM BUDDIES

An adventure to the great outdoors is featured in Megan's photos accented by punched and pieced "classmates." Begin by cropping photos into rectangles and ovals; mount on background of patterned paper (Creative Imaginations). Cut title banner using wavy ruler; double mat, trimming the first mat with decorative scissors. Adhere sticker letters (Sandylion). Use a jumbo circle punch to form children's "heads." Freehand cut "hair" and trim with a variety of decorative scissors; layer atop heads. Complete page with pen stroke details on "faces," journaling and photo captions.

Photos Megan Bennett, Denver, Colorado

Design Stacey Shigaya, Denver, Colorado

Take Our Daughters to Work Day

DOCUMENT A VALUABLE EXPERIENCE

An enriching day for Cheri's daughter "at the office" was documented with pride. Crop and silhouette photos; mount on patterned paper (Masterpiece Studios) background. Mount certificate and event artwork. Crop text block; add border punch (Family Treasures) details and journaling.

Cheri O'Donnell, Orange, California

Lindsey's Story, 6th grade

As a sixth-grader, Lindsey visited the Florida Keys with her summer school class. She took many pictures of the memorable trip. Lindsey cleverly displays her landlubber photos above a sticker "sea level" and her underwater photos below.

"I wanted to include my photos on a page in a unique way, so I decided to make half of my page look like it was water," says Lindsey. "I cut out some of the underwater pictures like fish to make them look like they were swimming under water!"

Lindsey Sebring, Sebring, Florida

Celebrations

In celebrating moments large and small, children learn how to invite joy into their lives. As important as marking holidays and birthdays is the simple revelry in finding how sweet ice cream tastes dripping down your arm. Saved treasures from celebrations help us remember the past and build our hope for the future.

Jammie Day
ENHANCE THEME WITH PAPER DOLLS

Cindy created a bedtime thematic page for photos taken at her daughter's kindergarten pajama day. Begin by cropping photos; round corners. Mat on patterned (NRN Designs) and solid paper. Create bedtime scene with paper dolls, pillow, teddy bear and book (EK Success), layered with die-cut bed (Stamping Station). Detail die cuts with pen and chalk. Complete page with die-cut title letters (Accu-Cut) cut from patterned paper (NRN Designs). Mat letters and silhouette; mount on page. Add journaling in white ink to finish.

Cindy Roberts, Bel Aire, Kansas

Here's the Scoop!
CHRONICLE A DELICIOUS DAY

Cindy captured the fun and delight of building sundaes at an ice-cream social at her daughter's school. Begin by mounting triangles on opposite corners of the page. Crop photos; use template (Creative Memories) for special shape and round corners. Mat photo; mount all photos on page. Draw title words and artwork with pen. Complete page with pen details and journaling.

Cindy Kacynski, Superior, Colorado

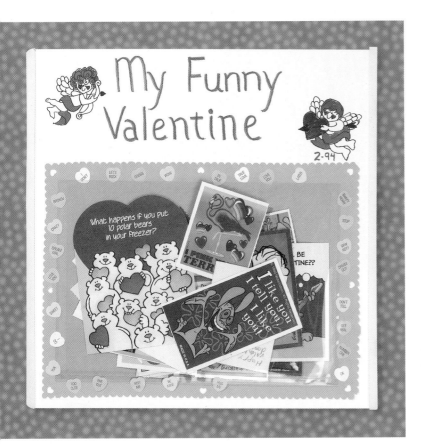

My Funny Valentine

PACKAGE A POCKET FULL OF CARDS

Cheryl preserved the fun and good feelings associated with her daughter's Valentine's Day party, even without a photo from the event. Begin by mounting a clear memorabilia sleeve (Creative Memories) to solid paper; trim paper with decorative scissors. Punch mini hearts at each corner. Adhere sticker hearts (Mrs. Grossman's) around sleeve. Draw and color cherubs. Complete by writing title with pens and inserting valentine cards.

Cheryl Padia, Riverside, California

Valentine's Day

PUNCH A SWEET VALENTINE'S TREAT

Alison created a box of candy conversation hearts spilling around a sweet-faced valentine. Begin by trimming cardstock 1" from the bottom with decorative scissors (All Night Media). Punch mini heart and dot to resemble lacy design. Mount 1½" strip of white cardstock behind punched design. Crop photos into circles and heart with template (Family Treasures); double mat, trimming with decorative scissors (Frances Meyer). Freehand cut candy box from cardstock. Punch jumbo heart (Marvy/Uchida); adhere vellum behind punched shape to create window. Punch small hearts from a variety of pastel colors; layer behind box and across page. Punch jumbo hearts from vellum. Finish page with journaling and pen stroke details.

Alison Beachem, San Diego, California

St. Patrick's Day 2000 – Jordan's class had a St. Patrick's Day Contest...Who could make the most interesting "Shamrock Poster"? Each child brought "green" items from home, and their teams decorated their "Shamrock Posters" and the class voted. Everyone wore green, and at the end of the day there was a great party to celebrate! There were green Jolly Ranchers, Green Jelly Beans, Green Sour Apple Candies (Mom's favorites!) and Shamrock Cookies. There were yummy cupcakes with green sprinkles, and Mrs. Brezden-Toney made her famous punch, which of course, was green!

Shamrock Shenanigans
PAPER PIECE A LUCKY LEPRECHAUN

Inspired by the luck of the Irish and a home-decorating magazine, Michele captured the fun of a St. Patrick's Day celebration at her son's school. Begin by chalking vertical lines 1½" apart to add dimension to solid background paper. Crop photos and round corners; mat on green paper. Paper piece an original leprechaun design and draw with chalk and pen strokes. Punch shamrock with jumbo heart punch (McGill); layer and mount on page. Punch jumbo squares (Family Treasures) for title block; adhere sticker letters (Frances Meyer). Complete page with computer-printed journaling.

Michele Weinberg
San Juan Capistrano, California

Party Theme Album

DOCUMENT HOLIDAY CELEBRATIONS

At no other time during a child's education are there more holiday parties than in grade school. Linda preserved her child's festivities in a school days album, which was part of a tribute to her child's beloved teacher, Mrs. Bochiechio.

The wide array of patterned papers and holiday-theme stickers, die cuts, stamps and punches available make it easy to create party pages. Note the patterned paper back grounds used on the "Spring Party" and "Trick or Treat" pages shown here. Linda takes advantage of the shapes in patterned papers by cropping the shapes out and placing her candid photos behind the paper—a great way to frame photos without adding extra bulk to a scrapbook album.

With a little creative cropping of your own, your classroom party pages will be something to celebrate!

Linda Foster, Williamsville, New York

"LE LION EST MORT CE SOIR"....

PETITS LIONS ET OURS

A LA FÊTE DE LA JUNIOR SCHOOL 1999

EMILIE ET SES COPAINS

LUDIVINE, AURELINE,

ALIX, FLORENCE, ALIZEE, C

Castille's Halloween Parade

INCORPORATE DESIGN INSPIRATIONS

Jeanne seeks inspiration for her pages wherever she can...even if it's from a design she sees on a piece of clothing! Crop photos, round corners. Mat on patterned papers (The Paper Patch). Adhere sticker letters (Frances Meyer). Layer die-cut stars (Ellison) on page; detail with pen strokes.

Jeanne Ciolli, Dove Canyon, California

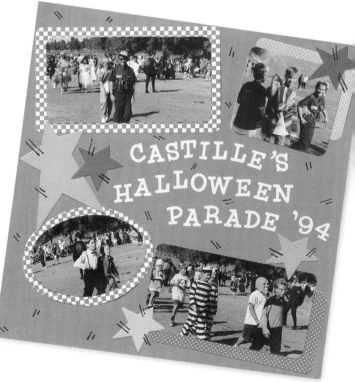

CASTILLE'S HALLOWEEN PARADE '94

Le Lion
CRAFT A COSTUME BACKGROUND

Natalie captures a fun day of dress-up with her wild, paper-crafted animal face. Begin by freehand cutting yellow and brown paper to resemble a wild and woolly mane; layer over solid background paper. Crop two photos into circles; mat on solid paper and layer over large white ovals for eyes. Slice panoramic photos into $1\frac{1}{8}$" strips; mount over eyes. Freehand cut muzzle, nose and eyebrows. Slice $\frac{1}{4}$" paper strips, trimmed with decorative scissors for whiskers. Freehand craft mouth and teeth; layer photos behind teeth. Complete with journaling on whiskers with white pen.

Natalie Papin, Arnas, France

Thanksgiving Feast
PRESERVE PRECIOUS HAND PRINT

Wendy found a special way to preserve her daughter's handprint and thankful words from a school Thanksgiving feast. Begin by drawing pen stroke border with ruler for guide around pages. Stamp fall designs (Stampin' Up!); color and detail with watercolor pens. Crop artwork with decorative scissors (Family Treasures). Mat handprint and artwork on cardstock textured with paper crimper (Fiskars). Add raffia bow. Crop photos; mount on page. Complete page with title and journaling.

Wendy Rueter
Rancho Santa Margarita, California

The Big Feast

DOCUMENT A DAY'S EVENTS

Susan and her daughter's kindergarten class gathered together for a traditional Thanksgiving feast, complete with pilgrim and Native American costumes made by the students. Adhere border stickers (Me & My Big Ideas) at bottom of pages. Crop photos and mat. Write title and mat. Frame title block with harvest stickers (Me & My Big Ideas). Complete page with journaling and photo captions.

Susan Brochu, East Berlin, Connecticut

november 24, 1999

THE BIG FEAST

You model your homemade vest and headband.

Both morning kindergarten classes celebrated Thanksgiving together with a big feast in the cafeteria. Places were set with placemats you had decorated yourselves, and the menu included fruit cup, homemade corn, pumpkin and cranberry breads and milk. Each student chose whether to dress as a pilgrim or a Native American. Since I was one of the room parents for your class, I was able to help with the festivities (and I brought my camera, of course!).

Maggie, Lia, Julia, Ambyr, Melissa & Shane

Almost time to dig in!

We thank you, LORD, for all these blessings...for family and friends and turkey dressing.

Your placemat

One more picture & then you can eat!

Melissa, you, Daniel & Jordan

"Smile and say 'We're stuffed!'"

Gingerbread House Party

ASSEMBLE A YUMMY COLLECTION OF TREATS

Alison features the edible tools of the trade that her son used to make his first gingerbread house. Double mat patterned paper (Making Memories) for background. Crop photos; single and triple mat on solid paper. Cut title letters using template (Scrap Pagerz); detail with chalk. Print rest of title words and photo captions from computer; cut to size and mat. Crop rectangles from brown cardstock; detail with chalk and colored pencils to resemble graham crackers. Crop "gumdrops" from colored paper; sponge stamp with white ink (Tsukineko) for sugary effect and layer at top and bottom of pages. Mount red cording (Darice) to look like licorice by stitching an "X" at loops.

Alison Beachem, San Diego, California

Field Days

On your mark, get set, GO! What a great celebration of athletics field days are, blending the salty taste of sweat with the sweetness of fresh air, friendly competition and laughing so hard it hurts. Blue ribbons, winners' medals and photos of friends and rivals make great displays to mark these glorious, heart-pounding days.

Juarez Olympics
SHOW ACTION WITH PAPER DOLLS

Michele documented her son's unique "Olympic" activity at school, using muted background colors and paper dolls to highlight event activities. Begin by matting white cardstock over gray cardstock, leaving ½" border. Crop and mat photos; mount on page. Computer journal title and text block on vellum; layer over gingham paper (Close To My Heart) and mat. Using a circle cutter, cut circles, then overlap and interlock as shown to create Olympic rings. Create paper dolls with template (Close To My Heart) and design outfit to match photos; detail with pen and chalk. Complete pages with pen lines around edges.

Michele Rank, Cerritos, California

Franklin School Field Day

FEATURE AN INTERESTING POINT OF VIEW

Lorna shows the fun of field day from the ground's point of view, featuring knobby knees and laced-up sneakers. Layer solid green cardstock over a 3½" strip of blue cardstock for the background. Mount school die cut (Ellison) and school bus and tree stickers (Mrs. Grossman's) to complete the background. Copy and size the leg and sneaker patterns (see page 120) to fit page. Cut pieces and assemble. Add texture to white paper with crimper (Fiskars) for socks. Adhere apple stickers (Mrs. Grossman's) and detail shoes with pen stroke details. Crop photos; mat a few and layer on page. Adhere title sticker letters (Creative Memories); layer with school-theme stickers (Mrs. Grossman's). Complete page with journaling.

Lorna Dee Christensen, Corvallis, Oregon

Field Day

RE-CREATE PARTICIPANT AWARDS

An award-winning day of fun and friendly competition is reflected on Rosemary's page full of ribbons. Crop photos; round corners and mat a few. Freehand cut awards using decorative scissors (Fiskars) for ribbon ends. Adhere sticker letters (Frances Meyer) and star stickers (Mrs. Grossman's). Complete with photo titles written on banner stickers (Frances Meyer).

Rosemary Palawski, Davison, Michigan

Awards & Ceremonies

Ceremonies and awards serve to honor not just achievement itself but also the hunger and hope to try. Invitations, programs and certificates are naturals for preservation and display in scrapbooks; they remind children of when they reached for the stars and, for a grand moment, touched one.

SEAN, 3RD GRADE

Erin's Awarding Year
PHOTOCOPY SCHOOL CERTIFICATES

Tami shows her daughter's "awarding" year with a page full of reduced copies of certificates earned. Punch award die cut (Ellison) on background paper; mount yellow cardstock behind to show through. Reduce color copies of certificates; cut to size and mount. Mat school portrait; trim with decorative scissors. Punch stars; mount on page. Complete page with journaling on award.

Tami Comstock, Pocatello, Idaho

D.A.R.E. Graduation
PRESERVE A PROUD MOMENT

Mary features her daughter's completion of the D.A.R.E. program along with her fifth-grade class. Cut two sheets of colored paper in half diagonally with decorative scissors (Fiskars) to form large triangles; mount on page as shown. Adhere border stickers (Mrs. Grossman's) at upper and lower page edges. Crop photos; mat or outline with stickers. Add program, sticker and journaling to complete.

Mary Browder, Shreveport, Louisiana

Approved Workmen Are Not Ashamed
CREATE AN AWARD-WINNING LAYOUT

Jolene captures her daughter's award-winning smile and achievement by re-creating the red ribbon awards on her page. Begin by drawing three horizontal lines across the top of the page. Circle-cut photos to look like medallions, focusing on award winners. Mat and add gold pen stroke details. Cut red cardstock into long "V" shapes to look like ribbons; detail with gold pen. "Hang" ribbons with medallions at the bottom from third horizontal line. Silhouette-crop photo and add title with pen at top of page. Complete page with journaling.

Jolene Philo, Boone, Indiana

Kindergarten Awards
SHOW OFF SCHOOL ACHIEVEMENTS

Rhonda captured her son's proud smile after he earned two special kindergarten awards. Start by drawing title frame and border; layer over background paper (Keeping Memories Alive). Triple mat photo; mount over ribbons. Complete page with paper doll (EK Success) dressed in clothes to match the photo.

Rhonda Scott, Fairfield, California

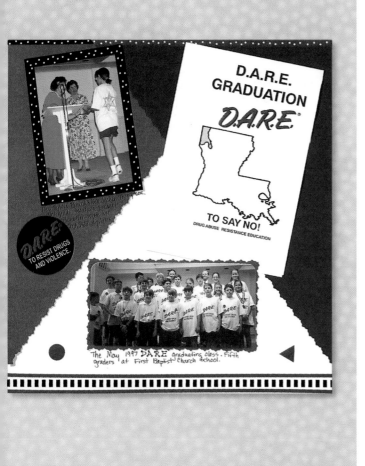

Graduation

All at once a child is not just a person and a classmate but a member of the "Class of..." Graduation ceremonies make this rite of passage real, complete with all the pomp and circumstance. Tassels, programs autographed by classmates and photos make great pages to remember this special time.

You're a Star!

PRESERVE A SPECIAL DOCUMENT

Debbie documents her son's rite of passage from elementary school to middle school with a star-studded layout. Begin by triple matting patterned paper (Stamping Station) for the background. Crop photos and double mat. Reduce and color copy diploma. Craft paper doll (DJ Inkers); detail with pens and chalk. Adhere shadowed sticker letters (Making Memories) to white paper strip. Mount to page with eyelets (Magic Scraps); detail title block with pens. Draw stars, silhouette; add details with pens. Mount to page with foam spacers (All Night Media).

Debby Schuh, The Memory Bee
Clarence, New York

Celebrate

PAY TRIBUTE TO GRADUATES

Narda captures the excitement of a spirited graduating class with bright colors and decorative pen work. Begin by cropping photos into rectangle and oval shapes; mat one photo. Freehand cut graduation caps; detail with pen. Triple-mat title block on solid and patterned paper (Provo Craft). Use decorative ruler as a guide for text written in a wavy fashion; pencil large letters around smaller words. Use two pen colors for lettering; add star and dot details on title block and around photos. Complete page with journaling.

Narda Poe, Midland, Texas

Little Huskies

SILHOUETTE PHOTOS OF FRIENDS

Carole gathered a number of graduation photos of her daughter's friends and silhouette-cropped them to fit on a one-page layout. Begin with a large, colored triangle layered with patterned paper (Hot Off The Press) for the background. Mount silhouette-cropped photos. Add die-cut heart (Creative Memories), title and journal quote.

Carole Parma, Albuquerque, New Mexico

Diploma

LAYER DIE-CUT ENHANCEMENTS

Jeanne assembled fun and colorful elements to reflect the joy of her son's sixth-grade graduation. Begin by silhouetting and cropping photos; triple mat on solid and patterned paper (The Paper Patch). Layer photos on page with computer-generated "diploma" and graduation cap die cuts (Ellison). Adhere graduation-theme stickers (Frances Meyer) on background and photos. Complete page with freehand-drawn lettering and pen stroke details.

Jeanne Ciolli, Dove Canyon, California

Graduation Day

FEATURE CLASSMATES' SIGNATURES

Tami documents her son's kindergarten graduating class with his classmates' signatures surrounding his handmade bear. Mount artwork at center of page. Crop individual signatures and mat; mount on page in random fashion. Adhere sticker letters (Creative Memories) and graduation cap stickers (Mrs. Grossman's). Finish page with journaling.

Tami Emricson, Woodstock, Illinois

Rachel's in the News!

FILL A POCKET WITH MEMORABILIA

Karen collected her daughter's fifth-grade awards, newspaper clippings and special keepsakes in a pocket page emblazoned with positive headlines. Create pocket page by cutting cardstock to one-half the height of page. Apply adhesive to three sides of cardstock, leaving the upper edge open to form pocket. Silhouette-crop "5th grade" title (Cock-a-Doodle Design) and images; mount on cardstock and mat. Circle-crop photo, adhere sticker letters (C-Thru Ruler) and insert memorabilia to complete page.

Karen Regep Glover
Grosse Pointe Woods, Michigan

Grad

FEATURE GRADS IN OVERSIZED CAP

Debi created a full-page smiling graduate to display photos of
a grade school graduation. Begin by layering patterned paper
(The Paper Patch) over white, leaving a ¼" border. Freehand cut
large circle and hair; detail with pen and chalk. Cut an 8" square
from black paper for back of graduation cap; layer behind head,
overlapping corner behind page. Crop photo using semi-circle
template (Puzzle Mates); mat on black paper and mount over
hair to complete cap. Add freehand-drawn tassel and diploma.
Crop second photo; triple mat. Punch stars (Family
Treasures). Complete page with title letters cut from template
(Puzzle Mates); mat on yellow paper and silhouette.

Debi Adams for Puzzle Mates, Anaheim, California

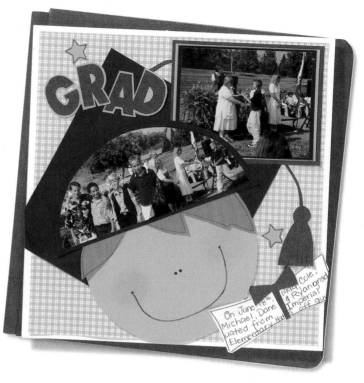

Kindergarten, Class of 2001

DRESS DOLLS TO DOCUMENT MILESTONE

Michele captures the pride and excitement her son experi-
enced at his kindergarten graduation with a succession of
celebratory paper dolls. Begin by layering patterned paper
(Close To My Heart) trimmed with decorative cutter
(Fiskars); layer over speckled background paper (Close To
My Heart), leaving ⁵⁄₁₆" border. Add pen stroke lines around
wavy border. Print title and journaling; trim and triple-mat.
Crop photos and double- or triple-mat. Craft paper dolls
and clothes with stencils (Close To My Heart). Stamp faces
(Close To My Heart); add chalk and pen stroke details.
For "diploma," roll paper scrap, flatten and glue together.
Adhere small paper strip to look like diploma tie.

Michele Rank, Cerritos, California

 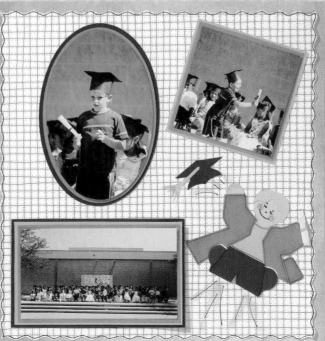

Casey

Casey was adorable in the dress that I made for her first day of school at Turtleback Elementary. She was so excited to start school. Special memories of this year were: her best friend Joy, her wonderful teacher Mrs. Brown, Pajama Day, Farmer Day and art time. 1995

Portraits & Milestones

"EDUCATION IS FOR

IMPROVING THE LIVES OF

OTHERS AND FOR LEAVING

YOUR COMMUNITY AND WORLD

BETTER THAN YOU FOUND IT."

—*Marian Wright Edelman,*
author (1939-)

There they are: the whole class and teacher together, every hair combed into place, just perfect. Captured on film are friends for a lifetime. Creating pages to display class and individual portraits helps to mark the passage of time. Eager yet timid preschoolers cross that threshold into kindergarten, then blossom with each passing year, laying the foundation for all learning that life will bring. Scrapbooking about a child's elementary years will help you remember, of course. But it also helps a child to build self-esteem. Kids see how our culture honors and remembers great leaders with formal portraits.

How fitting, then, to display children's portraits in scrapbooks. For they too will soon take their place in history.

JOSH, 2ND GRADE

CASEY
(SEE PAGE 125)

BIG USES FOR SMALL PORTRAITS

Try these fun and creative uses for those tiny photos that come in professional portrait packages:

• Add to a growth "timeline" to document grade school years.

• Add to mini "filmstrip" made with paper and filmstrip border punch.

• Create a shaped photomontage, like the schoolhouse to the right.

• Crop or stack and use to spell out child's name or age.

• Frame a large portrait with them.

• Make personalized greeting cards with them.

• Place in windows of paper-pieced schoolhouse or bus.

• Punch with a large shape punch and use for a border or corner design.

• Silhouette-crop photos and tuck into paper-pieced designs.

• Silhouette-crop photos and use for border.

• They are the perfect size for creating "family trees."

• Trim edges with decorative scissors to make a "postage stamp" for a school collage.

• Use to create the School Days page shown on page 122.

DYLAN, 2ND GRADE

Josh

PIN UP A SELF-PORTRAIT

Lori adds a fun element to her son's school portraits by posting a self-portrait that her son drew next to his individual portrait. First, crop and round corners of cardstock "bulletin board." Mount individual portrait and child's drawing; add pushpin stickers (Stickopotamus). Mat and mount class portrait; add pushpin die cut (Ellison) to complete page.

Lori Crain, Kent, Washington

Kendra in Kindergarten
FEATURE FULL-LENGTH PORTRAIT, TOO

Both casual and formal portraits of Dawn's daughter wearing her favorite dress on photo day come together in a simple layout. Begin by cropping photos; double mat on solid paper. Add detail with chalk around edges of second mat; mount on patterned background paper (Karen Foster Design). Tape embroidery floss (DMC Corp.) to backs of matted photos. "Hang" framed photos under silver fasteners (Westrim Crafts) mounted to page. Print title letters on computer; add color with chalk.

Design Brandi Ginn, Lafayette, Colorado

Photos Dawn Mabe, Broomfield, Colorado

Grant
DETAIL A MONOCHROMATIC BORDER

Barbara pieced together a detailed border to highlight a special nephew's school portrait. Begin by triple-matting portrait on solid and patterned (Keeping Memories Alive) papers. Cut photo corners with decorative scissors (Fiskars); mount matted photo on paper (Keeping Memories Alive). Begin border by cutting upper and lower center rectangles; double-mat. Crop rectangles for sides of the border; single- and double-mat. Draw title letters with template (The Crafter's Workshop); outline with pen and color in with pencils. Adhere school theme stickers (Creative Imaginations). Slice ¼" paper strips; tie and mount on page. Freehand draw and cut crayon box; color with pencils and chalk. Finish with journaling block.

Barbara Otten, Durand, Michigan

Adding Eyelets

One of the latest hardware crazes to find its way into our scrapbooks is eyelets—little, one-piece metal fasteners that you apply to the page with an eyelet setter and a craft hammer. Eyelets work well for both masculine and feminine pages, such as this school portrait of a young girl. Eyelets can be left unadorned or laced with ribbon, raffia, metallic cord or natural jute, depending on the look you wish to achieve.

Kindergarten picture • Teacher: Mrs. Campaglio • Friends: Sage, Lily, Courtney, Savannah, September 2000

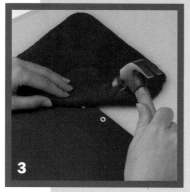

1 *Use a ⅛" round hand punch to punch two holes in cardstock that you will use for photo mat's background (Figure 1).*

2 *Turn cardstock over and push the elongated, tubular end of eyelet into punched hole from the front of the cardstock. Place cardstock, with eyelet tube facing up, on a craft mat. Insert eyelet setter into eyelet's tube and strike the top of the eyelet setter a few times to flatten tube (Figure 2).*

3 *Turn cardstock over to its front. Cover eyelet with a soft cloth to protect it from scratches, then strike the eyelet with a hammer again one or two times to "finish the set" and further flatten out the eyelet (Figure 3).*

Shannon

ADD A DAINTY TOUCH WITH EYELETS

Liz pulls an element from her daughter's red-bowed dress onto a photo mat with the use of eyelets and ribbon. Begin with child's name cut from template (Cut-It-Up) on patterned paper (The Paper Patch), matted and adhered across top of page. Add double-matted journaling block across lower edge of page. Follow the steps at left to attach eyelets to background of photo mat. Double mat photo and accent with punched daisies; draw pen stroke details on daisy petals and add punched circles at daisy centers. Insert ribbon into eyelets; tie in a bow. Mount matted photo to page to finish.

Liz Connolly, Sturbridge, Massachusetts

ENLISTING YOUR CHILD'S HELP TO MAKE PHOTO MATS

Looking for a creative way to spend time with your child and preserve memories at the same time? Enlist your child's help in creating photo mats for his or her school portraits. You will both enjoy these project ideas:

• Punch out or cut many different-sized shapes from bright-colored cardstock and make a collage. See page 90 for using tiny portrait "postage stamps" in your collage.

• Give your budding artists lots of drawing paper and acid-free pens so that they can create their own masterpieces for photo mats or frames.

• Remember how much fun you had sprinkling glitter when you were a child? New, acid-free glitter glues can give your child the same fun without the mess. They are great for making abstract designs on photo mats.

• Everybody loves stickers! Make a fun border using favorite stickers.

• Press your child's hand onto a washable ink pad, and have him make handprints on paper. Keep plenty of moist wipes on hand to clean up any excess ink left on his fingers.

• Children love to collect things. Take them on a nature hike and have them gather leaves, flowers, stones or seashells. Scan a photo of these items into your computer, and print out a mat featuring your child's favorite things!

• Provide your child with large die cuts and let her decorate them with chalk.

• What could be more fun than tearing paper into pieces and not getting scolded for it? Enlist your child's help in creating mats with torn edges by giving him cardstock and letting him tear to his heart's delight.

• Make bubble paper. Mix up some soap water with food coloring, give your child a bubble wand, and let her blow bubbles onto a piece of white cardstock. Cut the cardstock into mats.

• Have your child make patterned paper using rubber stamps, washable ink or markers or crayons.

Nicolas Paul Wilhite

FRAME A PORTRAIT WITH CHILD'S OWN ARTWORK

Charlotte's son was seven years old when he discovered fonts and was intrigued with them. Charlotte framed his school portrait with the "ABCs" written in various "fonts" by Nick.

Charlotte Wilhite, Fort Worth, Texas

Paper Folding

The wide array of school-theme patterned papers available makes paper folding a fun and unique way to accent school portraits. Paper folding, with its origins deep in the ancient art of origami, is easy to do. Just a few folds here, a few creases there and some creative assembly is all you need to do.

You can use many different folds. Here we feature the envelope fold. By assembling folded pieces into a ring, you can easily frame a portrait. Experiment by altering the number of folded pieces used to make squares, rectangles or smaller circles to frame photos.

For the folded frame shown here, you will need twenty-five 2¼" squares of patterned paper (Hot Off The Press). One 8½ x 11" piece of patterned paper will yield twelve squares. Fold each piece following the steps below. Try folding a few practice pieces first.

Nicky

FOLD A SCHOOL PORTRAIT FRAME

Folded school-theme papers add excitement to Andrea's page featuring her son's first-grade portrait. Begin with matted cardstock background. Circle-crop an enlarged photo into an 8" circle; mount at center of page. Add apple die cuts (Colorbök) and school stickers (Frances Meyer) to page. Fold pieces following the steps below and at right; then assemble pieces and mount on page. Add journaling to die cuts to finish page.

Andrea Price, Auburn, New York

Envelope Fold

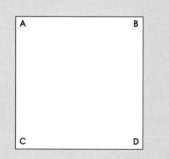

1 *Begin by cutting 2¼ x 2¼" squares from any style of lightweight paper. Cut a few extra for practice. On the backside of your practice square, label the corners with a pencil.*

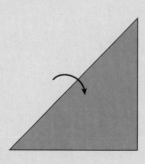

2 *Fold corner A to corner D and crease the diagonal edge.*

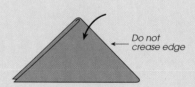

Do not
crease edge

3 *Fold corner B to C. Do not crease the edge.*

Assembly

Line up twenty-five folded paper pieces atop the circle photo's edge with even spacing, overlapping square, non-folded edges as needed to complete the circle. When you are satisfied with the placement and spacing of each piece, secure each piece in place with adhesive.

Paper folding technique by Kris Mason of Folded Memories and Laura Lees of L Paper Designs. For more on paper folding, see Memory Makers® Memory Folding™. *(Ordering information is on page 127.)*

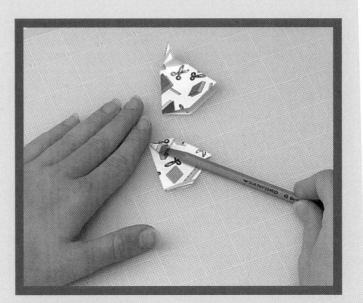

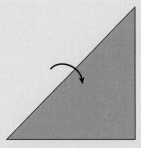

4 *Pinch top of triangle to create a center crease.*

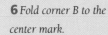

5 *Unfold square. (The creases are guidelines for the next steps.)*

6 *Fold corner B to the center mark.*

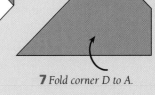

7 *Fold corner D to A.*

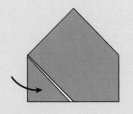

8 *Fold corner C to the center.*

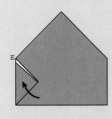

9 *Next fold back corner C to E.*

10 *Insert a pencil into the last fold to create a pocket (Figure 1).*

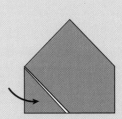

11 *Flatten the pocket to form a small kite shape.*

School Days

FEATURE CLASSMATE PHOTOS

Carrie, a first-grade teacher, documents her class's individual photos with handmade apples and the three "Rs": reading, 'riting and 'rithmetic. First, circle-crop photos. Adhere photos to various-colored, freehand cut and accented apple die cuts; set aside. Adhere cropped title and apples from patterned paper (Provo Craft) to page as shown. Journal around page edges. Place die-cut photo apples on spread in a carefree arrangement; mount in place. Add student names and small punched apples to finish page.

Carrie Davis, Everett, Washington

Ryan

USE HARDWARE FOR MASCULINE TOUCH

Liz's use of punched rectangles and brass fasteners lend a masculine touch to her son's school portrait. First, crop photo, round corners and double mat. Create photo border with punched rectangles (Family Treasures) layered on punched 1" squares (Family Treasures). Mat again; add decorative fasteners (Impress Rubber Stamps) to corners before mounting on page. Crop and double-mat paper for title block, add journaling and decorative fasteners to complete page.

Liz Connolly, Sturbridge, Massachusetts

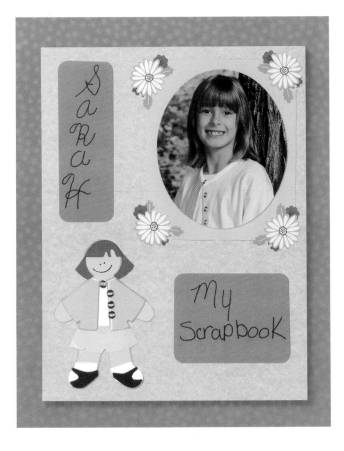

Sarah's Story, 3rd grade

Sarah—the third-grade scrapbooking sidekick of her mother, Megan—enjoys creating pages about her first day of school, field trips and her Halloween parade. One of her recent pages shows a paper doll dressed cleverly in the same outfit that Sarah is wearing for her school portrait.

"I thought it was a great 'picture day' outfit and I thought by doing the paper doll in a matching outfit, it would bring out the clothes I was wearing," says Sarah, who matched even the button details on her paper doll.

"I will pass my scrapbook on to my kids," she says. "They will be able to see what I looked like as a little girl and what my clothes and school looked like. My mom says it's important for my kids to see my handwriting, too."

Sarah Glynis-Margaret Bennett, Denver, Colorado

WORKING WITH HERITAGE PHOTOS

For an archival-quality album environment:

• Handle heritage photos with care; avoid direct light.

• Use non-permanent mounting techniques (photo corners, sleeves, etc.) for easy removal for copying or restoration.

• Keep cropping to a minimum; background objects tell their own stories of place and time.

• Do not trim or hand-tint old photos. Have reprints made first.

Carol Jo Gajewski
PRESERVE VINTAGE SCHOOL PORTRAITS

Christie created multiple monochromatic pages for her mother's priceless sepia-toned class photos. Mat photos on paper trimmed with decorative scissors (Westrim) with clear photo corners (3L); mount over patterned background paper (NRN Designs). Add vintage school theme stickers (NRN Designs) atop paper squares trimmed with decorative scissors. Create title block with sticker frame (NRN Designs). Finish with double-matted title block.

Christie Scott, Trevor, Wisconsin

Paper Silhouettes

PROFILE YOUR CHILD WITH A SILHOUETTE

Paper silhouettes are easy to make and add to any child's school days scrapbook album.

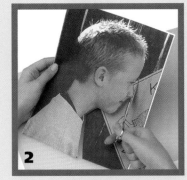

1 *Begin with a "profile" photograph that shows just head and shoulders. Photocopy the photograph, enlarging to desired size to fit intended space on a scrapbook page (Figure 1).*

2 *Cut out the photocopied profile, staying true to outlines of facial features and hair (Figure 2).*

3 *Place the cut out profile onto black paper and trace around it with a pencil (Figure 3).*

4 *Cut out the black paper silhouette and mount on a lighter, double-matted background if desired (Figure 4).*

*Photo MaryJo Regier
Littleton, Colorado*

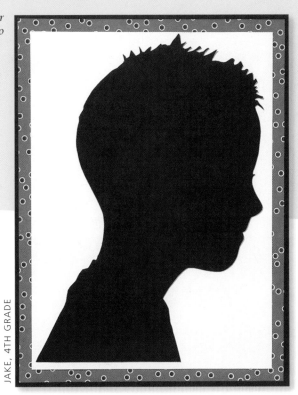

JAKE, 4TH GRADE

May '97

POST SIGNS ALONG THE ROAD TO LEARNING

Pamela looked no further than the background of her son's portrait for inspiration when creating a page border. Begin by slicing four 1½" wide strips of black paper; mount on page. Slice a yellow sticker strip (Mrs. Grossman's) at ¼" intervals and adhere down center of black border for road lines. Adhere road signs and bus stickers (Mrs. Grossman's) and sticker letter outlines (Creative Memories). Mount photo with clear mounting corners (Creative Memories).

Pamela Byrd, Huntsville, Alabama

School Days

FRAME A CLASS PHOTO

Keep the focus on a large class photo with a simple frame and background. Begin by framing a photo with a paper frame (Provo Craft). Add silhouette-cropped title and apples from patterned paper (Provo Craft) to keep the page clean and simple.

Joyce Schweitzer
Greensboro, North Carolina

Smile

SLICE A TITLE WITHIN A TITLE

Liz was inspired by her daughter's bright smile and so she titled the page accordingly! Begin by cropping photo; round corners and mat. Trim mat with decorative corner punch (All Night Media) and mat two more times. Punch smiley faces (Marvy/Uchida); mount on 1½" paper border strip. Add eyelets (Impress Rubber Stamps; see technique on page 92) to corners and detail with white pen. Create title block; cut letters from template (Scrap Pagerz). Slice letters horizontally; adhere to cardstock, leaving ⅜" space between letter pieces. Write title phrase and detail lines around edges.

Liz Connolly, Sturbridge, Massachusetts

Grade 4

FRAME PORTRAIT WITH CLASSMATES

Ardie framed her daughter's fourth-grade portrait with classmate photos cropped to fit a bold border. Begin by slicing two 2⅜" wide paper strips for the sides of the border and slice two 1½" strips for the upper and lower borders. Crop class photos into rectangles; mount as shown. Adhere title letters (Creative Memories) at top of page. Crop portrait; mat on patterned paper (Creative Memories). Complete with student and teacher names.

Ardie Clark, Eugene, Oregon

St. Walter's School of Religion
IDENTIFY CLASSMATES IN A PHOTO

With all of those class photos taken during school, it can be tricky to put names with faces as the years pass by. One simple solution is to create a diagram right on the scrapbook page to reference those in the photo.

Follow the instructions below to create a reference diagram. Then mount matted class photo, accented with handmade letters (see pattern on page 120), to page. Add page title and journaling in pen.

Photo Kimberly Ball, Denver, Colorado

St Walter's School of Religion

A B C D E F G H I J K L M N O P Q R S T U V W X Y Z

5th Grade   Room 8B

1989–1990

19- Mr. Herb Boehm
1- Clair Huber   2- Megan Buck   3- Kim Ball
4- Stacy Fischer   5- Julie Casek
6- Erin Cannella   7- Brooke Dennis
8- Josh Smith   9- Doug Kotlarczyk
10- Craig Smith   11- Scott Wolff
12- John Ypil   13- Joe Nowosielski
14- B.J. Natividad 15- Mike Nizzi
16- Stephanie Boehm 17- Michele Roberto
18- Michelle Lagdan

Make a photocopy of the photo, enlarging or reducing as needed to fit intended space on scrapbook page. Place white scrapbook page atop photocopy on a light box or bright window; moving photocopy around beneath page to find proper positioning. Use a pencil to trace outlines of each individual in photo directly onto scrapbook page as shown; retrace in black ink. Assign a number to each person in the diagram and list the numbers and corresponding names directly on the scrapbook page.

Portrait Theme Album

WATCH GROWTH WITH PORTRAITS

Sometimes it is hard to know what to do with all of those 8 x 10" portraits that come in portrait packages. Joyce creates a page for each enlargement to show a chronological progression of her daughter's school days growth.

Joyce's page design layouts enhance the portraits and are simple enough to keep from stealing attention away from the photos. The combination of bright and muted patterned papers and cardstock work together for a unified look, while different sticker, decorative scissors, punch and die-cut accents make each page unique.

This is a great way to scrapbook these wall-size portraits when they are taken down from the living room wall each year and replaced with a new school year portrait.

Joyce Schweitzer
Greensboro, North Carolina

Documenting the Difficult Times

Life's challenges are rarely the most fun times, but they are often
the most meaningful. Kids have a tremendous adaptability to
overcome obstacles. Mark their progress to show your support.
Remember that challenges are best met together.

Alina's Story, 2nd grade

As a toddler, Wendi's daughter was diagnosed "developmentally delayed" with low
muscle tone. Wendi and her husband spent
countless hours trying to inspire Alina to use
a crayon on paper. "Finally, she did begin...
and creating art for herself and for others
has been her favorite pastime for years,"
says Wendi.

By age six, Alina was diagnosed as mild-
ly autistic with continued low muscle tone. Today, with a
loving family and a home program called Applied Behavior
Analysis or ABA, she thrives beautifully with a little extra
support in a regular class. She also participates in Girl Scouts
and is on a summer swim team.

Alina says, "I like to scrapbook every day!" She is as
familiar with Wendi's scrapbook supplies as her mother is.
"Sometimes I remind her of the steps (select pictures, paper,
stickers, etc.), which helps her with her independent-type
skills," says Wendi. "Then Alina is left to create. The only
requirement is that she writes on each page."

Through scrapbooking and living with a special-needs
child, Wendi has learned how to tell history and cherish
today as it is. "This is our life and
even though we believe Alina will overcome her autism, the
road she and the family have traveled is important and
needs to be embraced in our family history."

For Alina, scrapbooking allows her to express her likes,
dislikes and how she perceives her world. "It's a way to
communicate through art," says Wendi. "Alina's fine motor
skills have improved significantly using cutters, punches,
scissors and stickers. You know how hard they are to get
just where you want them!"

Alina and Wendi Hitchings
Issaquah, Washington

A New School

SOFTEN THE BLOW OF A NEW SCHOOL

Alex used a photocopy of her daughter's favorite new shirt, complete with "pop-dotted" hula skirts, to document her start at a new school in Hawaii. Begin by adding matted border strips to page edges. Crop and mat photos, adhere as desired. Add child's drawing and matted journaling blocks. Freehand cut and adhere title lettering. Accent pages with chalked punched shapes (EK Success, Family Treasures, McGill) to finish.

Alexandra Bishop, Honolulu, Hawaii

My Son, My Hero

JOURNAL A SPECIAL STORY

(BELOW) Kimberly titled her page to reflect the hard work and dedication her son put forth to overcome his learning disability. Freehand cut large book; mount layers over solid background. Cut title letters with template (source unknown) from solid and patterned (Northern Spy) papers. Circle-crop photo; mat for letter "O" in "son." Assemble paper doll (EK Success); detail with pen. Print journaling; crop and double mat. Reduce report card and certificate; double mat. Mount ribbon to page.

Kimberly Edwards, Jacksonville, Florida

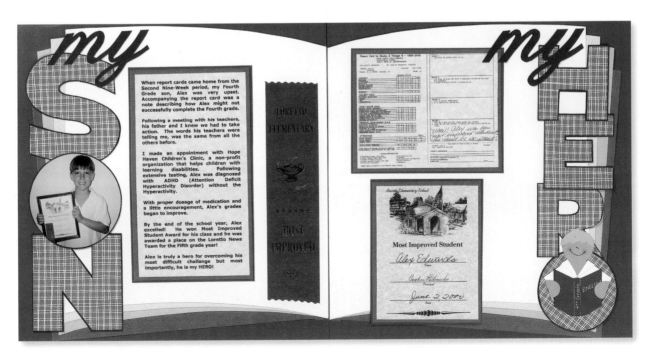

HELPING YOUR CHILD BUILD CONFIDENCE

Self-confidence helps children succeed in school. Self-confident children take risks that are necessary to try new things and be creative. Here are some ways to foster self-esteem:

• Teach children to respect themselves by treating them with respect. Listen to them and acknowledge their feelings.

• Accentuate the positive. Focus on children's unique interests and strengths and help foster them.

• Do not compare children with their siblings or classmates.

• Help children find group activities where they can make friends with other children who share their interests.

• Teach children how to set realistic goals for themselves. Break down goals and tasks into easy steps.

• Mistakes are not failures! They are simply opportunities to learn new skills. Give children the freedom to make mistakes.

• Provide lots of encouragement and celebrate life's little victories.

• When criticism is necessary, provide feedback that is specific to the children's actions.

• Don't criticize the child as a whole person.

• Give choices so that children develop a sense of independence and accountability.

• Allocate responsibility. Give children age-appropriate chores and tasks to foster a sense of responsibility.

• Be consistent. Foster children's sense of trust and safety by setting fair and reasonable boundaries.

Proud to Be Me

DOCUMENT A CHILD'S CONFIDENCE

Kathy found herself smiling at her son's answers to a class assignment, so she made a copy of his work and created a page reflecting his healthy self-esteem. Begin by cropping school pages and matting with decorative scissors (Fiskars) and corner rounder. Mount extra school photos down side of page; complete page with sticker letters (Making Memories) and monster stickers (Mrs. Grossman's).

Kathy Thomas, Fairfax Station, Virginia

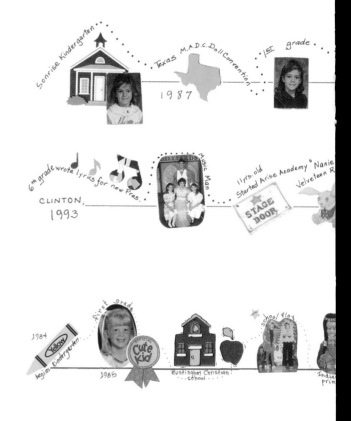

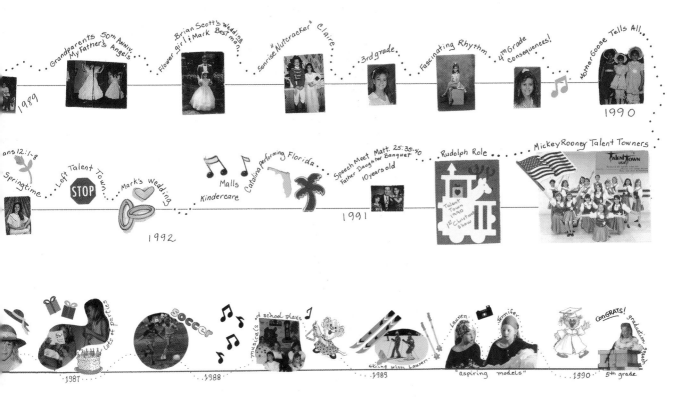

Grandparents 50th Anniv. My Father's Angels • 1989 • Brian Scott's Wedding Flower girl & Mark Best man • Sunrise "Nutcracker" Claire • 3rd grade • Fascinating Rhythm • 4th Grade Consequences! • Mother Goose Tells All • 1990

ans 12:1-8 Springtime • Left Talent Town • STOP • Mark's Wedding • Kindercare Malls • Catalina performing Florida • 1991 • Speech Meet Matt. 25:35-40 Father Daughter Banquet 10 years old • Rudolph Role • Talent Town 1990 1st Christmas Show • Mickey Rooney Talent Towners • 1992

Lots of parties • 1987 • Soccer • 1988 • Musicals and school plays • Skiing with Lauren • 1989 • Lauren • Jennifer • "aspiring models" • ConGRATS! graduation speech • 1990 • 5th grade

Grade School Timelines
SHOWCASE ELEMENTARY HIGHLIGHTS

Naomi (UPPER) and Barbara (LOWER) capture the growth and activities that their children experienced during their elementary school years with small photo vignettes and a variety of stickers on a comprehensive timeline. Although these timelines are shown as one continuous line, adjust the number of lines across your page to accommodate the amount of your child's "highlights." Begin making a timeline by drawing horizontal lines 1¾" apart.

Silhouette-crop photos and place along freehand-drawn timeline, leaving room for stickers (Bo-Bunny Press, Frances Meyer, Mrs. Grossman's, Sandylion, Suzy's Zoo) and journaling. Assemble and arrange all photos and stickers along timeline before adhering to page to ensure adequate spacing. Finish with journaling.

Naomi Paris, Covina, California

Barbara Wegener, Huntington Beach, California

My Class

FOLD OUT AN INTERACTIVE "YEAR IN REVIEW"

It is almost unbelievable how much happens in just one school year! Nevertheless, with creative page additions and creative cropping, Oksanna managed to feature her son's entire 1999/2000 school year in an amazing two-page spread. Exact instructions for this incredible scrapbooking fete will depend upon what you wish to include, but here is some insight to perhaps inspire you to try this.

Start with a four blank scrapbook pages—two will be the base "spread" and the two in the center are cropped in half horizontally, one forming a fold out pocket. Attach more pages with artist's tape to the outer edges of your base spread to create a "gate fold," if desired. From here, the world is your stage! Read on the next page for all of the little "interactions" that Oksanna built into her "Year in Review."

Oksanna Pope, Los Gatos, California

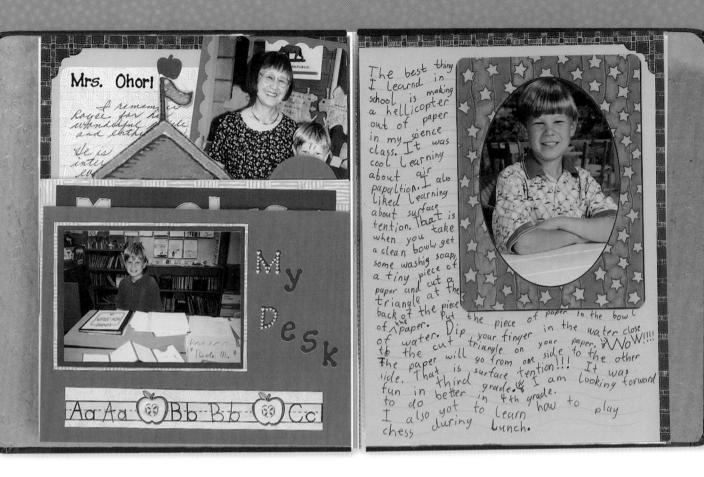

Oksanna uses a whole rainbow of complementary-colored papers for backgrounds and photo mats and an assortment of school-theme borders, stickers, die cuts and punched shapes for accents. Enlarged die cuts are adhered to page edges to create foldouts and one cropped center page becomes a pocket for holding her son's report card.

The photos and journaling work in unison to tell the story of the school year. Topics include projects, a note from Royce's teacher, a carpool schedule, his daily school activities, a class photo with classmate names, and a letter from Royce about what he learned in third grade. This unique spread scores an "A+"!

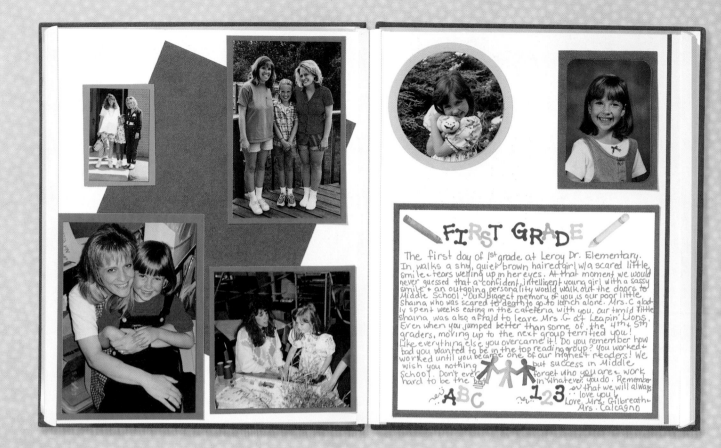

Student Appreciation Theme Album

PRAISE A JOB WELL DONE

When grade school gave way to middle school, Tracy enlisted the help of her daughter's grade school teachers to create a "continuation" gift album for Shaina. Before she left school for summer break, Shaina and her mom visited with all of her past teachers. Tracy took candid student/teacher photos and secretly left blank white note cards and an acid-free pen with each teacher, along with a little note asking them to write Shaina a letter.

The letters, often quite touching, provide a moving documentation of Shaina's learning experience and growth during the grade school years. Some people got very creative—such as the Before and After School program director

that Shaina would help instead of going outside for recess; she wrote her letter in rebus journaling, shown above. The letters were matted and mounted on scrapbook pages, along with the photos and simple school-theme stickers.

The teachers were happy to oblige and the gift album has become very dear to Shaina as she moves on to the next phase of public education.

Tracy Johnson, Thornton, Colorado

SCRAPBOOKS IN THE CLASSROOM

Scrapbooks can enhance school curriculum because students learn in different ways, and scrapbooking allows for that individuality. Many teachers, like Shelley Balzer, have found fun and innovative ways to use scrapbooks in the classroom. "The kids will say they like the stickers best, but really, looking at the completed project over and over again is the best part," she says.

Some teachers also use scrapbooks in the class-room to encourage writing, preserve a school's history; present a class project (see pages 44-45); document a year of studies, field trips and events; show student pen pals in other countries what school life in America is like; and more.

Shelley Balzer, Bakersfield, California

Teacher Appreciation Theme Album

CRAFT A GIFT FOR A #1 TEACHER

To help celebrate Teacher Appreciation Day in her child's kindergarten class, Nancy enlisted the help of the classmates to create a special ABC album to present to Mrs. Cole.

"I mailed blank scrapbook pages to all the kids in the class to do their own page at home," says Nancy. To compensate for the children who did not return a finished page, she made a basic scrapbook page with each child's name and some colored pen strokes on it. The kids wrote a letter to Mrs. Cole and drew pictures on their pages.

"Mrs. Cole was absolutely thrilled with the book," says Nancy. "She had no idea what we were doing, but she had wondered why I came to school and took some odd pictures—like the one of the kids all hopping like frogs—which was the class mascot."

Nancy's ABC gift album includes a year of memories: the names and photos of all of the classmates, class parties and activities, thank you letters from the children, field trips, certain classes and curriculum—even a personalized pop-up decorated with an assortment of die cuts!

Nancy Picogna, Cullman, Alabama

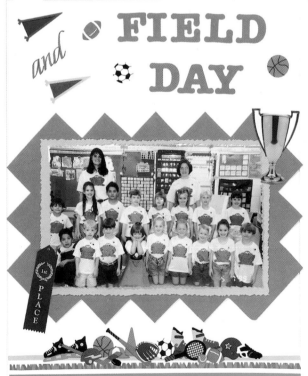

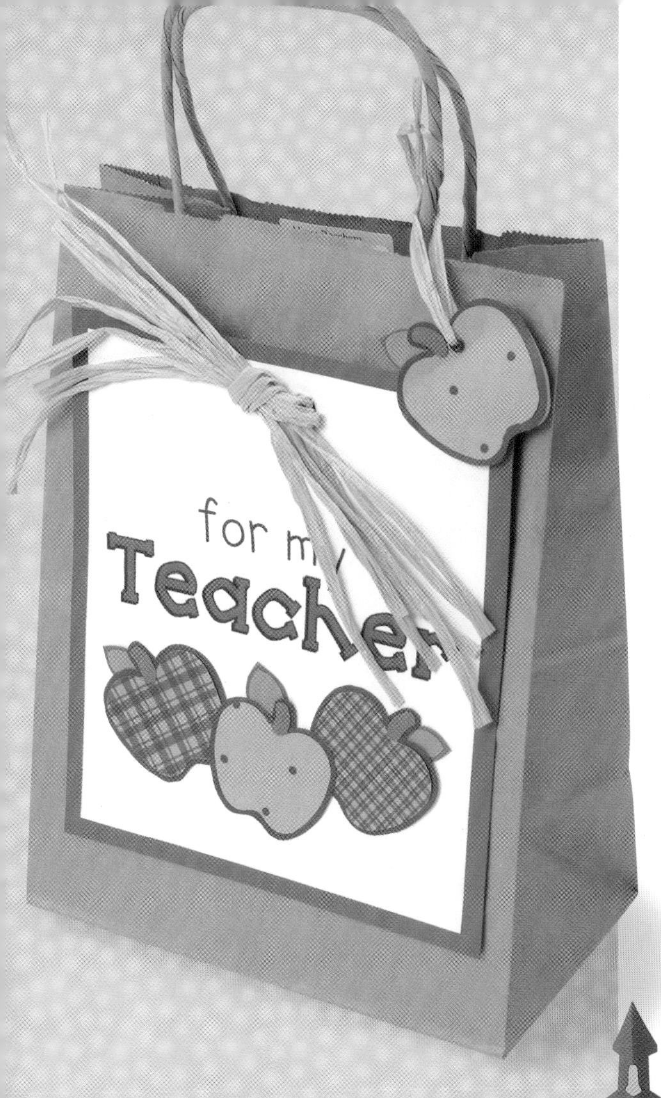

Gift Bag

PRESENT GIFT ALBUM IN STYLE

Should you decide to help your child's class make a Teacher Appreciation Album for the end of the school year, why not present it in a handmade gift bag—such as Alison's punch art gift bag shown at the left? Begin with a plain or colored, undecorated gift bag large enough to hold the gift album. Computer-print gift tag onto white cardstock and mat. Punch holes in top of large gift tag; insert raffia, tie in knot and adhere to bag. Accent tag with super jumbo punched apples (Marvy/Uchida) from patterned papers (Making Memories); mat with paper and adhere. Add an eyelet (see page 92) to one additional matted apple and dangle from handle on another strip of raffia.

Alison Beachem, San Diego, California

Note: We have included a pop-up pattern on page 120 so that you can make your own school-theme pop-up page. Simply decorate the pop-up with your own silhouette-cropped photos, stickers, die cuts, punch art or embellishments.

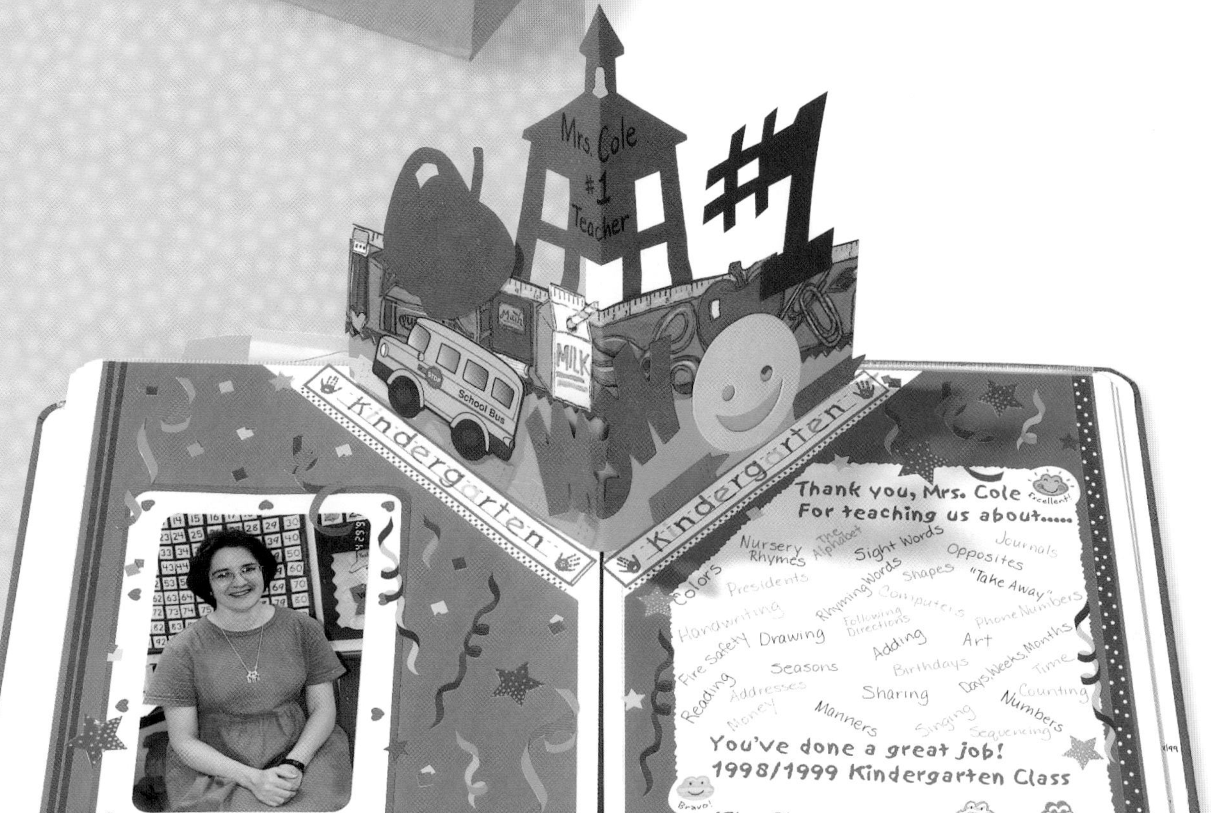

Miss Kimmie and Miss Joanne were Blair's teachers and she loved being in their class.

Andrea's teacher was Mrs. Lorenz and she was fortunate to have her for both kindergarten and 1st grade!

School was Cool but now we're...

OUT!

The kids were so excited to be out of school that they came home and celebrated by dressing up for the occasion. Blair shows off her new shoe ornament and Andrea writes a letter to Mrs. Lorenz thanking her for being such a great teacher.

School Was Cool

PAPER PIECE A CHALKBOARD

Cindy's kids met the last day of school with the same excitement as the first day. Crop photos; mat on black paper. Print journaling on computer; cut to size and mount. Make chalkboard by mounting ½" strips of patterned paper (Provo Craft) around edges of black rectangle. Write title with chalk (Craft-T Products) using a pointed cotton swab. Cut rest of title letters from template (EK Success); mat and silhouette. Add journaling.

Design Brandi Ginn
Lafayette, Colorado

Photos Cindy Kacynski
Superior, Colorado

School's Out for Summer

USE PAPER SCRAPS FOR TITLE LETTERS

The last day of school always brings a familiar song to Karen's mind, so she built a page around its title. Begin by layering red cardstock over white, leaving ¼" border. Crop photos; single- and double- mat on patterned (Bazzill) and solid papers. Draw title letters (source unknown) with pencil; cut paper scraps to fit wide section of letters from patterned paper. Adhere scraps and outline letters with red pen. Double-mat title block. Journal on apple die cut (Ellison); mat and silhouette. Complete page with sticker numbers (C-Thru Ruler).

Karen Regep Glover
Grosse Pointe Woods, Michigan

1999

school's out for Summer

Say Bye to Grade Five
PAY TRIBUTE TO A TEACHER

Terri pays tribute to one of her daughter's favorite teachers with last-day-of-school photos. Crop photos into shapes; trim rectangle with corner rounder and mount all on page. Draw grid lines using ruler as guide with pens. Stamp various designs and title letters (Close To My Heart); color with pens. Draw detail lines around photos and journal to complete page.

Terri Howard, Hood, California

End of Year
LAYER A DIE-CUT BORDER

Joyce highlighted her daughter's favorite classmates by layering circle-cropped faces onto a colorful die-cut border that resembles a paper doll chain. Add die-cut paper dolls (Crafty Cutter) across lower edge of page; add circle-cropped photos of children for faces. Crop and mat large photos into ovals with decorative scissors (Fiskars). Freehand draw title block paper "pin ups" and "pushpins," and mount sticker letters (Creative Memories) in squares. Stamp yellow stars (All Night Media). Finish with pen stroke border and journaling.

Joyce Schweitzer, Greensboro, North Carolina

Quotes & Sayings

Give your scrapbook pages an inspirational or comical lift with these quotes and sayings about school days, teachers and learning. For more quotes, see those featured at the beginning of each chapter on pages 15, 35, 55 and 89.

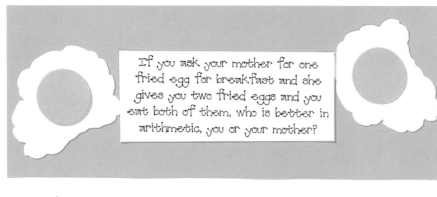

A child's mind is like a shallow brook which ripples and dances merrily over the stony course of its education and reflects here a flower, there a bush, yonder a fleecy cloud...
—*Helen Keller*

A child's life is like a piece of paper on which every person leaves a mark.
—*Chinese proverb*

A good education is the next best thing to a pushy mother.
—*Charles Schultz*

A teacher affects eternity; he can never tell where his influence stops.
—*Henry Brooks Adams*

A teacher can but lead you to the door; learning is up to you.
—*Chinese proverb*

Children are young, but they're not naive. And they're honest. They're not going to keep awake if the story is boring. When they get excited you can see it in their eyes.
—*Chinua Achebe*

Tracy Johnson, Thornton, Colorado
Quote by Carl Sandberg, 1878-1967

Education is not preparation for life; education is life itself.
—*John Dewey*

Good teachers are usually a little crazy.
—*Andy Rooney*

I always tell students that it is what you learn after you know it all that counts.
—*Harry S. Truman*

It is a glorious fever, that desire to know.
—*Edward Butler Lytton*

Learning how to learn is life's most important skill.
—*Michael Gelb and Tony Buzan,* Lessons from the Art of Juggling: How to Achieve Your Full Potential in Business, Learning and Life

Learning is at its best when it is deadly serious and very playful at the same time.
—*Sarah Lawrence Lightfoot*

Let us tenderly and kindly cherish, therefore, the means of knowledge. Let us dare to read, think, speak and write.
—*John Adams,* Dissertation on the Canon and Feudal Law

People seldom see the halting and painful steps by which the most insignificant success is achieved.
—*Annie Sullivan*

The experience gathered from books, though often valuable, is but the nature of learning: whereas the experience gained from actual life is of the nature of wisdom.
—*Samuel Smiles*

The human mind is our fundamental resource.
—*John F. Kennedy*

The important thing is not so much that every child should be taught, as that every child should be given the wish to learn.
—*John Lubbock*

The world exists for the education of each [person].
—*Ralph Waldo Emerson*

To be able to learn is to be young, and whoever keeps the joy of learning in him or her remains forever young.
—*J.G. Bennett*

To me education is a leading out of what is already there in the pupil's soul.
—*Muriel Sparks*

There are two kinds of teachers: the kind that fills you with so much quail shot that you can't move, and the kind that just gives you a little prod behind and you jump to the skies.
—*Robert Frost*

We cannot always build the future for our youth, but we can build our youth for the future.
—*Franklin D. Roosevelt*

Lettering Patterns & Page Title Ideas

Use these convenient lettering patterns to add a fun finishing touch to your grade school pages. Simply photocopy the lettering pattern, scaled to the size you need, and trace onto your page in pencil using a light table or window. Retrace and color in pen color of your choice. Or make your own patterns from the page title ideas listed by theme.

BACK TO SCHOOL

Back-to-school blues
Back-to-school shopping madness
Be true to your school
Bus stop
Catching the bus
First day jitters
First day of school
Getting ready
Getting started
Is summer over already?
My backpack
My school
Our school rocks!
Rise and shine!
School bus
The shopping experience
Special school clothes
The Pledge of Allegiance
Wake up, wake up, wake up!
Waking up

ALL IN A DAY'S WORK

#1 Kid
#1 student
#1 teacher
1st place
A day in review
A few of my favorite things
A typical day
Be true to your school
Best friends
Best friends forever
Lunch
The lunch bunch

My favorite lunch
My favorite teacher
On the playground
Our children, our future
Proud to be me
Recess
Recess fun
School days
School daze
School is cool
School spirit

ACTIVITIES & SPECIAL EVENTS

4-H
The big feast
Celebrate!
Costume parade
Crossing over
Graduate of 2009
Graduate of 2010
Graduate of 2011
Graduate of 2012
Graduate of 2013
Graduate of 2014
Graduate of 2015
Happy Valentine's Day
Holiday brunch
Holiday party
Ice-cream social
It's cookie time!
Jammie day
My funny Valentine
My merit badges
News flash
On my honor
Our Christmas party
Our fundraiser
Pomp and circumstance
School news
School program
Scout's honor
Shamrock shenanigans
Spring fling
Student of the month
Thanksgiving feast
We're so proud!
What a genius!

ACADEMICS

Computer whiz
Everything I Need to Know I Learned in…
Field trip
Geography
Gym
Hard at work
Home school is cool!
Homework blues
Homework is fun—NOT!
Honor roll
Honor student
I love reading
Mad science
Making the grade
Mathematical genius
Now that's teamwork
Our little Einstein
Our Picasso
Physical education
Readin', 'ritin', 'rithmetic
Reading rules!
Science fair
Science project
Spelling bee
Spelling champ
Summer school
What a fine artist!
What I learned
The world is our classroom

PORTRAITS & MILESTONES

A new school
Back 2 school
Congratulations!
D.A.R.E. graduation
End-of-year party
Glad grad!
Graduation day
Here's looking at you, kid
Here's to the Graduate!
Hollywood smile
Jr. High, here I come!
Last day of school
Look at me now!
Middle school, here I come!
Middle school rules!
My diploma
No more pencils, no more books
Our shining star
Pomp and Circumstance
Proud to be me
Say "Cheese"
School's out for the summer
School was cool, but now we're out!
See you in September
Watch me grow!
The year in review
You ought to be in pictures

PERFORMANCES

A note-able performance
A sparkling performance
A star is born
A stellar performance
Born to dance
Curtain call
It's show time
Keepin' the beat
Making music
Musical celebration
My recital
The world's a stage
You're a star!

SPORTS

All star
First and ten
Goal!
Little league champs
Put me in coach, I'm ready to play
Take me out to the ballgame
There's no "I" in "teamwork"
You did it!

Project Patterns

Use these helpful patterns to complete specific scrapbook pages featured in this book. Enlarge and photocopy the patterns as needed to fit your photos and/or page size.

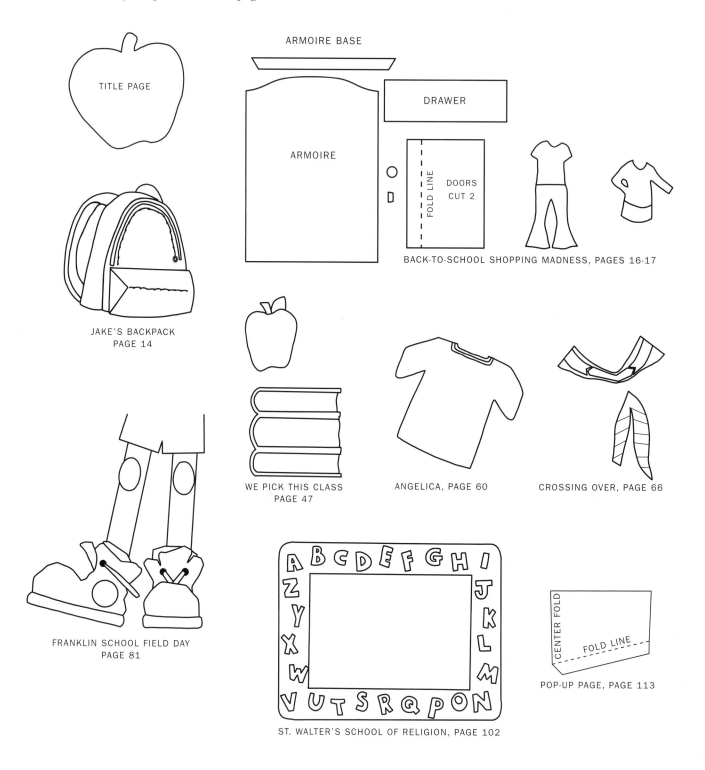

TITLE PAGE

ARMOIRE BASE

DRAWER

ARMOIRE

DOORS
CUT 2

FOLD LINE

BACK-TO-SCHOOL SHOPPING MADNESS, PAGES 16-17

JAKE'S BACKPACK
PAGE 14

WE PICK THIS CLASS
PAGE 47

ANGELICA, PAGE 60

CROSSING OVER, PAGE 66

FRANKLIN SCHOOL FIELD DAY
PAGE 81

ST. WALTER'S SCHOOL OF RELIGION, PAGE 102

CENTER FOLD

FOLD LINE

POP-UP PAGE, PAGE 113

Paper Piecing Patterns

To incorporate your own photos into these original paper-pieced designs, photocopy and enlarge the patterns below to fit your selected photos. Cut the pattern pieces apart, transfer the pieces to colored or printed papers of your choice and cut out. Reassemble all elements, adding a silhouette-cropped photo to complete the design.

TITLE PAGE

PAGE 13

PAGE 3

PAGE 15

PAGE 5

PAGE 35

PAGE 37

PAGE 41

PAGE 40

PAGE 40

PAGE 82

PAGE 55

PAGE 89

PAGE 126

Page Patterns

Our ready-made patterns make it easy to begin a portrait, vital statistics or autographs scrapbook page. Simply enlarge to 120% (for an 8½ x 11" page) or 135% (for a 12 x 12" page) and photocopy onto desired paper; then add cropped photos or journaling.

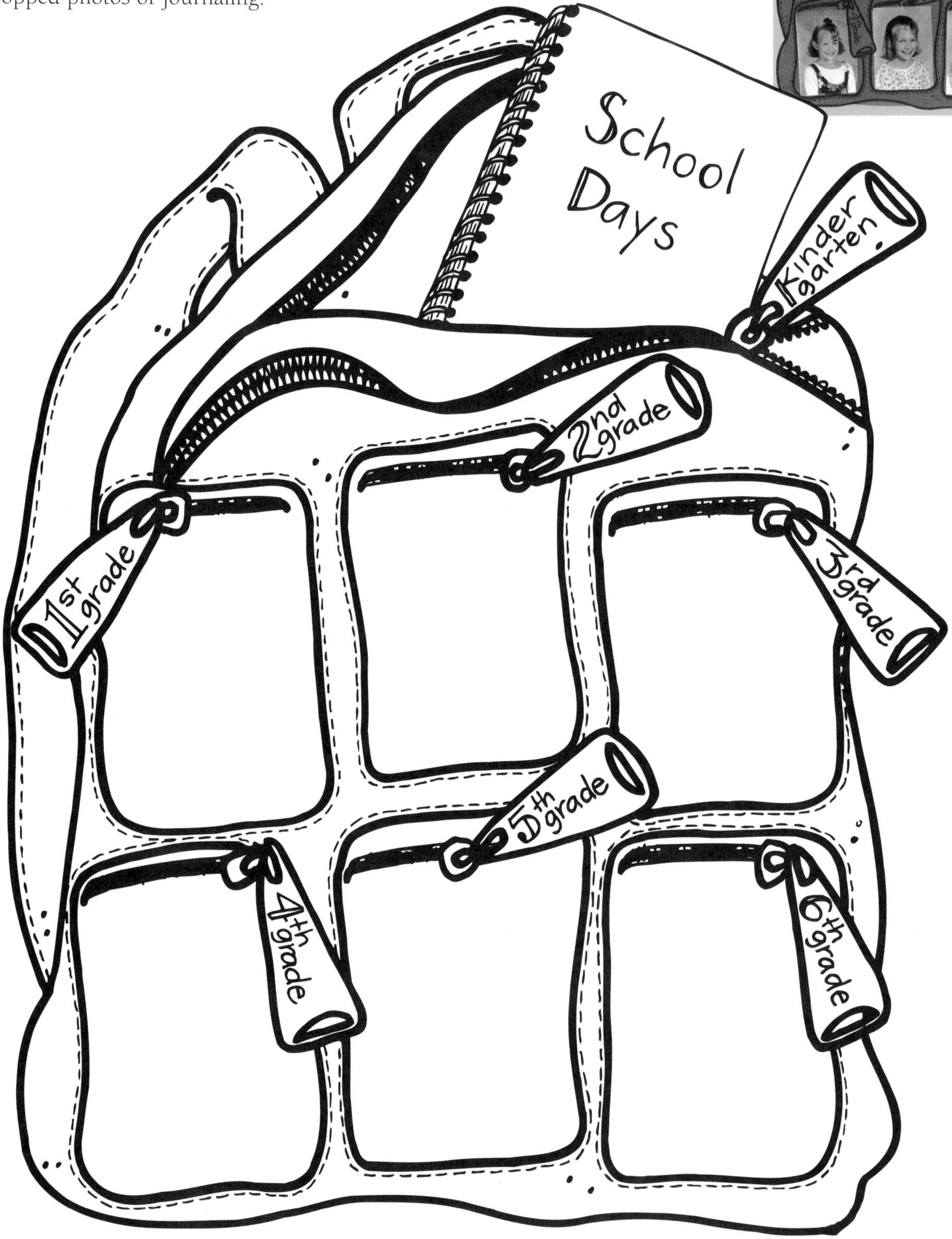

School Days

Kindergarten

1st grade

2nd grade

3rd grade

4th grade

5th grade

6th grade

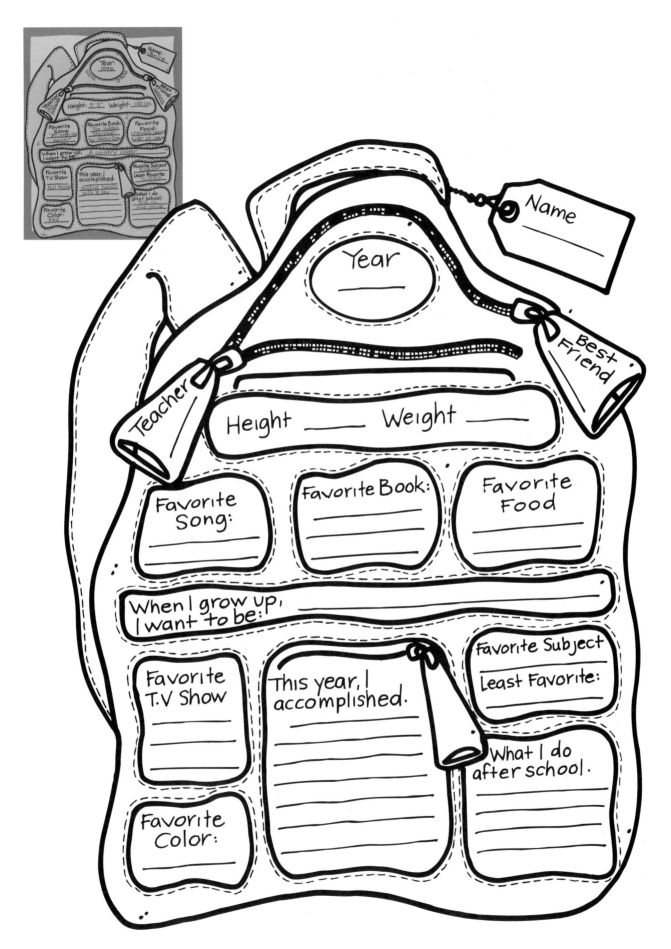

Name
_____

Year
_____

Best Friend

Teacher

Height _____ Weight _____

Favorite
Song:
_____
_____

Favorite Book:
_____
_____

Favorite
Food
_____
_____

When I grow up,
I want to be: _____

Favorite
T.V Show
_____
_____

This year, I
accomplished.
_____
_____
_____
_____

Favorite Subject
_____
Least Favorite:
_____

What I do
after school.
_____
_____
_____

Favorite
Color:
_____
_____

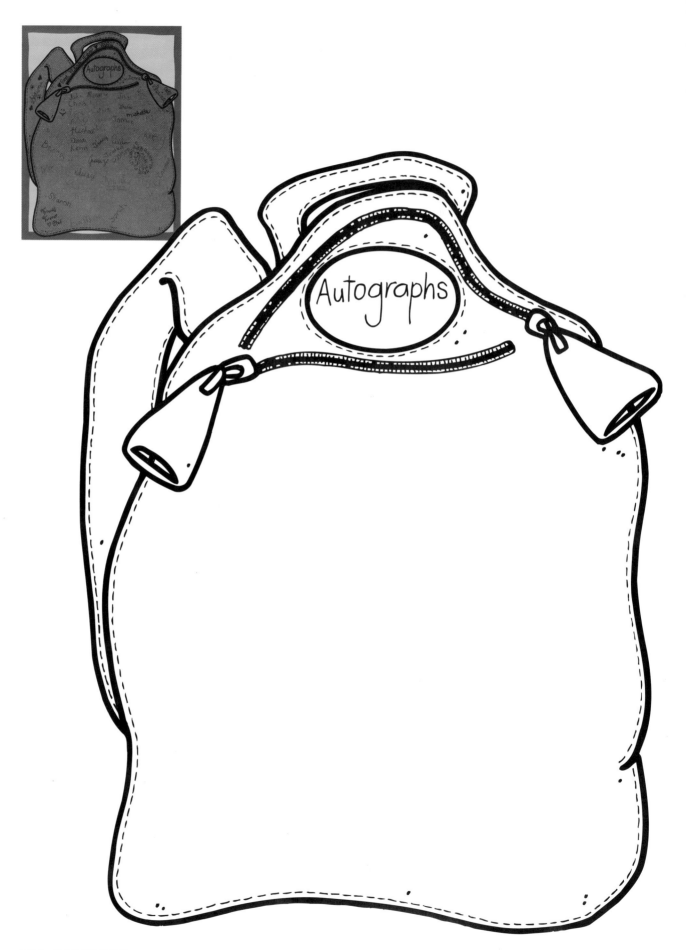

Instructions & Credits

cover, page 88
Casey

Irma's flair for detail and design in the clothes that she makes for her daughter is reflected on a page decorated with school day symbols. Begin by mounting large portrait. Slice ½" strip of solid paper; mount below photo. Cut rectangle from vellum for title block; mat on solid paper. Cut letters from templates (C-Thru Ruler, EK Success). Use craft knife to cut letter "a" out of apple die cut (Provo Craft); mount solid paper behind letter before mounting on page. Cut ten 2⅛" squares from solid and patterned papers (Making Memories, Paper Adventures, Provo Craft). For left border, cut vellum to size of square and adhere with eyelets (Impress Rubber Stamps); slip small photo in pocket. Punch medium apples (HyGlo/American Pin); mount over square with self-adhesive foam spacers. Draw letters on next square. Cut apple from template (source unknown) with craft knife; mount over solid paper. Adhere sticker letters (Making Memories) for lower square. For right border, cut letter "C" using template (C-Thru Ruler); layer over patterned paper. Draw letters on next square with white pencil; layer apple die cut (Provo Craft) over squares. Mount die-cut apple on next square with foam spacers. Draw letter "a" with template on patterned paper. Print journaling on vellum; mount over last two squares. Mount all squares on page in topsy-turvy fashion. *Design Pam Klassen; Photos Irma Lozano-Gabbard, San Diego, California*

page 6
Our Little Artists

Creativity and art plays a major role in the lives of her family, so Michele makes sure to feature her kids' artwork whenever possible. Frame the page by drawing a wavy border with decorative ruler (C-Thru); cut out, crimp (Paper Adventures) and slice ends at an angle where corners meet; mount over solid background paper. Crop photos; mount behind paper "frames." Slice strips for frame title plates; mount with eyelets (Impress Rubber Stamps). Mount eyelets to sides of frames; tie craft thread (DMC Corp.) to eyelets.

Mount eyelets to page to "hang" frames, looping thread under eyelet to secure. Create title letters with pen; color with pencils and adhere sticker letters (Mrs. Grossman's). Complete page with journaling. *Design Ann Kitayama, Broomfield, Colorado; Photos Michele Gerbrandt*

page 14
Jake's Backpack

MaryJo captured in photos the best part of starting the school year to her son—buying new school supplies and a new backpack to carry them in—and saved her least favorite part: the receipt! Paper tear a 2 x 2½" strip from the top and bottom of a 12 x 12" cardstock; layer over solid background paper as shown, leaving space between torn strips. Double mat photos; mount on page. Print journaling from computer; mount on page. Punch large rectangles (Family Treasures) in various colors; layer at top of page, over photos and on text block as shown. Cut title letters from template (C-Thru Ruler); mat and silhouette. Layer first letter of each word on large rectangle. Paper piece backpack (see page 120 for pattern). Add detail with metallic thread (Kreinik), ribbon (C.M. Offray & Son), eyelets (Creative Impressions) and cording (source unknown). Complete page with hidden school supply receipt; fold "accordion-style" under triple-matted text block. *Design Pam Metzger, Boulder, Colorado; Photos MaryJo Regier, Littleton, Colorado*

page 34
The Science Fair

Pennie's son enjoyed the success of a science experiment that led him to a district science fair. Crop and partially silhouette photos; mat two photos on solid and patterned (Paper Adventures) papers. Cut large circle and ring from solid and patterned paper; layer over patterned background paper (Paper Adventures). Freehand draw and cut title banner from vellum and mat. Adhere sticker letters (Stickopotamus); write subtitle. Complete page with journaling; mat and mount on page. *Pennie Stutzman, Broomfield, Colorado*

page 54
Lady Storm

A colorful combination of patterned paper sets the stage for Narda's action photos. Begin by cutting patterned papers (Paper Fever) along design lines; mount at upper and lower edges of page over red patterned paper (Scrapbook Wizard). Crop photos and mat on solid paper. Cut title and journaling block; add freehand-drawn decorative lettering, pen stroke stitching and freehand-drawn soccer ball. Freehand cut lightning bolt from patterned paper (Scrapbook Wizard). Detail with chalk to complete page. *Narda Poe, Midland, Texas*

PHOTOGRAPHING MEMORABILIA

A picture of your child's sports, club and activities memorabilia gets those items into the scrapbook without adding bulk. Try these great tips:

- Memorabilia can include uniforms, equipment, trophies—even shoes!

- Outdoors, use 200-speed film and flash; shoot in open shade or soft sunlight.

- Indoors, use 400-speed film and flash; shoot in well-lit location or late in the day for a nostalgic effect.

- Arrange memorabilia on floor or tabletop in an eye-pleasing display.

- Fill the frame with your arrangement when you look through the camera's viewfinder.

- Get in as close as possible to accurately record words and numbers.

- Snap many photos from different angles, rearranging memorabilia as needed for greater visual appeal.

- For a photography alternative for flat memorabilia such as ribbons and certificates, scan the item(s) into your computer, either alone or in collage-style, reduce the size, and print on acid-free paper of choice.

Page Contributors

Adams, Debi 87
Angard, Kelly 28, 56
Asher, Pat 62
Babbitt, Nadine 21
Badgett, Susan 24
Balzer, Shelley 111
Barlow, James William III 44
Beachem, Alison 48, 49, 73, 79, 113
Bennett, Sarah 97
Bilash, Maggie 64
Birkhead, Gail 66
Bishop, Alexandra 105
Bleicher, Alexandra 49
Bowders, Lori 68
Brochu, Susan 78
Brookins, Kerri 32
Browder, Mary 83
Byrd, Pamela 100
Carey, Joy 26, 30
Christensen, Lorna Dee 81
Ciolli, Jeanne 62, 67, 76, 85
Clark, Ardie 101
Commons, Donna 67
Comstock, Tami 83
Connolly, Liz 92, 97, 101
Crain, Lori 90
Davis, Carrie 96
Delavan, Cheryl 61
Dougherty-Wiebkin, Sabina 18
Edwards, Kimberly 105
Emricson, Tami 86
Fenton, Donna 46
Foster, Linda 75
Frye, Pamela 40
Garner, Marilyn 38
Gerbrandt, Michele 6
Ginn, Brandi 91, 114
Glover, Karen Regep 33, 42, 66, 86, 114
Gould, Kym 67
Graham, Lorie 65
Gray, Cathy 57
Hitchings, Alina 104
Holland, Patti 63
Howard, Terri 115
Johnson, Tracy 110-111, 116
Johnston, Joellyn Borke 59
Kacynski, Blair 39
Kacynski, Cindy 72
Kitayama, Ann 6, 90
Klassen, Pam 12, 88
Langhans, Lisa 61
Lindner, Kathleen 16-17
Lomax, Jacquie 69
McElfresh, Ann 38
McGoveran, Angie 30
McKenna, Sarah 63
McWhorter, Heather 58, 64
Meerschaert, Tammy 56
Metzger, Pam 14
Moll, Jennifer 31
Moxley, Amy 53
Naylor, Helen 41
Newton, Angela 65
Noren, Adrian 51

O'Donnell, Cheri 71
Otten, Barbara 91
Padia, Cheryl 73
Palawski, Rosemary 81
Papin, Natalie 76-77
Paris, Naomi 107
Parma, Carole 85
Peterson, Chris 47
Philo, Jolene 83
Picogna, Nancy 112-113
Pierson, Johnna 50
Pittard, Donna 19
Poe, Narda 54, 84
Pope, Oksanna 29, 32, 36, 42, 65, 69, 108-109
Price, Andrea 94
Purnell, Gary 45
Quimbaya, Suzy 60
Rank, Michele 27, 80, 87
Rhoads, Melissa 28
Roberts, Cindy 72
Rognlie, Amy 36
Rueter, Wendy 77
Scamfer, Sally 23
Schuh, Debby 47, 84
Schweitzer, Joyce 18, 100, 103, 115
Scott, Christie 98
Scott, Rhonda 83
Sebring, Lindsey 71
Seydel, Susan 51
Shepherd, Heather 60
Shigaya, Stacey 70
Shute, Sue 41
Simmler, Diane 52
Smith, Theresa 46
Spurlock, Heather 20
Stutzman, Pennie 34
Swanson, Julie 22
Tardie, Chris 59
Thomas, Kathy 106
Trachtman, Kimberly 19
Vezeau, Rachel 21
Wegener, Barbara 107
Weinberg, Michele 74
Wendt, Gretchen 25
Wilhite, Charlotte 93
Wilson, Janna 26
Zieske, Johnny 43

Photo Contributors

Ball, Kimberly 102
Bennett, Megan 70
Brough, Dawn 8-12
Dollman, Phyllis 23
Gerbrandt, Michele 6, 55
Hawthorne, Lynn 37
Kacynski, Cindy 114
Landry, Maria V. 35
Lozano-Gabbard, Irma Cover, 88
Mabe, Dawn 91
Matt, Robin 15, 40
Neufeld, Jill 122
Perkins, Kris 89
Regier, MaryJo 14, 56, 90, 99
Scamfer, Sally 1, 126
Schuh, Debby 47
Stutzman, Pennie 82

Professional Photographers

cover, page 88 Casey
North Light Studios
14034 Poway Road
Poway, CA 92064

page 25 Kindergarten
Interstate Studio
819 S. Earl Ave.
Lafayette, IN 47904

page 26 Kindergarten
Jay Dee's Photography
108 Hwy 71 N, Suite 108
Alma, AR 72921

page 30 Second Grade
Verissimo Photography
P.O. Box 784
Visalia, CA 93279

page 56 Bear Creek Bears
Garris Photography
c/o Lone Bear Ranch
P.O. Box 158
Drake, CO 80515

page 89 Josh
Masterpiece Studios, Inc.
1722 Graves Court
Northglenn, CO 80233

page 90 Josh Crain
Buteau's Photography
150318 Military Rd. S
Suite 219
Seattle, WA 98188

page 91 Grant
Life Touch National School Studios
1716 West Milham Ave.
Portage, MI 49024

page 92 Shannon
Pavitt Photography
22 Old Village Road
Sturbridge, MA 01566

page 93 Nicolas
Glamourcraft School Division
5747 Westcreek Drive
Fort Worth, TX 76133

page 94 Nicky
CNY School Photography, Inc.
74 State Street
Phoenix, AZ 13135

page 97 Ryan
T.D. Brown by Lifetouch
1170 Pontiac Ave.
Cranston, RI 02920

page 97 Sarah
Lifetouch National School Studios
65 Betasso Road
Boulder, CO 80302

page 100 May '97
Larry Waldrup Photography
728 Arcadia Circle
Huntsville, AL 35801

page 101 Smile
Pavitt Photography
22 Old Village Road
Sturbridge, MA 01566

page 101 Grade 4
Lifetouch National School Studios
2089 Laura St.
Springfield, OR 97477

page 106 Proud to Be Me
Life Touch National School Studios
4515-D Day Drive
Chantilly, VA 20151

page 108 My Class
Lifetouch National School Studios
191 Stauffer Boulevard
San Jose, CA 95125

page 112 Field Day
Larry Waldrup Photography
728 Arcadia Circle
Huntsville, AL 35801

page 122 Backpack Portraits
Verissimo Photography Service
P.O. Box 784
Visalia, CA 93279

KARI, 6TH GRADE

Sources

The following companies manufacture products featured in this book. Please check your local retailers to find these materials. In addition, we have made every attempt to properly credit the trademarks and brand names of the items mentioned in this book. We apologize to any company that we have listed incorrectly or the sources were unknown, and we would appreciate hearing from you.

3L Corp.
(800) 828-3130 (wholesale only)

Accu-Cut
(800) 288-1670
www.accucut.com

All Night Media, Inc.
(800) 782-6733

Bazzill Basics Paper
(480) 558-8557

Beary Patch, The
(877) 327-2111 (wholesale only)

Bo-Bunny Press
(801) 771-4010 (wholesale only)
www.bobunny.com

Boy Scouts of America National Council
(972) 580-2000

Broderbund Software
(319) 247-3325
www.broderbund.com

Canson, Inc.
(800) 628-9283

Clearsnap, Inc.
(800) 448-4862
www.clearsnap.com

Close to My Heart
(888) 655-6552
www.closetomyheart.com

C.M. Offray & Son, Inc.
(800) 344-5533
www.offray.com

Cock-A-Doodle Design, Inc.
(800) 262-9727
www.cockadoodledesign.com

Colorbök
(800) 366-4660 (wholesale only)

Crafter's Workshop, The
(877) CRAFTER
www.thecraftersworkshop.com

Craf-T Products
(507) 235-3996

Crafty Cutter
(805) 237-7833
www.crftycttr.com

Creative Imaginations
(800) 942-6487

Creative Memories
(800) 468-9335
www.creative-memories.com

C-Thru Ruler Company, The
(800) 243-8419
www.cthruruler.com

Cut-It-Up
(530) 389-2233
www.cut-it-up.com

Darice, Inc.
(800) 321-1494

Design Originals
(800) 877-7820
www.d-originals.com

D.J. Inkers
(800) 325-4890

DMC Corp.
(973) 589-0606
www.dmc.usa.com

DMD Industries, Inc.
(800) 805-9890
www.dmdind.com

Doodlebug Design, Inc.
(801) 524-0050

Duncan Enterprises
(559) 291-4444

EK Success
(800) 524-1349
www.eksuccess.com

Ellison Craft & Design
(800) 253-2238
www.ellison.com

Emagination Crafts, Inc.
(630) 833-9521
www.emaginationcrafts.com

Family Treasures, Inc.
(800) 413-2645
www.familytreasures.com

Fiskars, Inc.
(800) 950-0203
www.fiskars.com

Frances Meyer, Inc.
(800) 372-6237
www.francesmeyer.com

Hambly Studios
(800) 451-3999
www.hamblystudios.net

Hot Off The Press
(800) 227-9595
www.paperpizzaz.com

Hyglo/American Pin
(800) 821-7125
www.ameripin.com

Impress Rubber Stamps
(206) 901-9101

Inkadinkado Rubber Stamps
(800) 888-4652
www.inkadinkado.com

It Takes Two
(800) 331-9843

Joyful Heart Stamps
(949) 770-7959
www.joyfulheartstamps.com

Judi-Kins
(800) 398-5834
www.judikins.com

Karen Foster Design
(801) 451-9779
www.karenfosterdesign.com

Keeping Memories Alive
(800) 419-4949

Kreinik Manufacturing Co.
(800) 537-2166

Magic Scraps
(972) 385-1838

Making Memories
(800) 286-5263
www.makingmemories.com

Marvy Uchida
(800) 541-5877
www.uchida.com

Mary Engelbreit Studios
(800) 443-6379

Masterpiece Studios
(800) 447-0219
www.masterpiecestudios.com

McGill Inc.
(800) 982-9884
www.mcgillinc.com

Me and My BIG Ideas
(949) 589-4607 (wholesale only)
www.meandmybigideas.com

MPR Associates, Inc.
(336) 861-6343

Mrs. Grossman's Paper Co
(800) 429-4549
www.mrsgrossmans.com

My Mind's Eye, Inc.
(801) 298-3709

Nankong Enterprises, Inc.
(wholesale only)
(302) 731-2995

Northern Spy
(530) 620-7430
www.nspycom

NRN Designs (wholesale only)
(800) 421-6958

Paper Adventures
(800) 727-0699
www.paperadventures.com

Paper Cuts
(800) 661-4399
www.papercuts.com

Paper Fever Inc.
(801) 412-0495

Paper Patch, The
(800) 397-2737 (wholesale only)

Pebbles In My Pocket
(800) 438-8153
www.pebblesinmypocket.com

Plaid Enterprises, Inc.
(800) 842-4197
www.plaidenterprises.com

Posh Impressions
(800) 421-7674

Preservation Technologies
(800) 416-2665

Provo Craft
(888) 588-3545

Pulsar Paper Products
(877) 861-0031

Punch Bunch, The
(254) 791-4209 (wholesale only)

Puzzle Mates
(888) 595-2887
www.puzzlemates.com

Ranger Industries, Inc.
(800) 244-2211
www.rangerink.com

Robin's Nest Press, The
(435) 789-5387

Rubber Stampede
(800) 423-4135
www.rubberstampede.com

Sandylion Sticker Designs
(800) 387-4215
www.sandylion.com

Scrapbook Wizard, The
(801) 947-0019

Scrapable Scribbles
(801) 255-5465

Scrap Pagerz
(435) 645-0696
www.scrappagerz.com

Sonburn, Inc.
(800) 527-7505
www.sonburn.com

Stampabilities
(800) 888-0321

Stampendous! (wholesale only)
(800) 869-0474

Stampin' Up!
(800) 782-6787
www.stampinup.com

Stamping Station Inc.
(801) 444-3828

Stamps N Memories
(909) 381-6063

Stickopotamus
(888) 270-4443
www.stickopotamus.com

Suzy's Zoo
(800) 777-4846
www.suzyszoo.com

Therm O Web, Inc.
(800) 323-0799

Too Much Fun Rubber Stamps
(517) 351-2030

Tsukineko, Inc.
(800) 769-6633
www.tsukineko.com

Westrim Crafts
(800) 727-2727

Windows Of Time
(801) 732-1053
www.windowsoftime.com

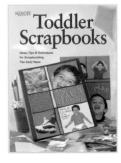

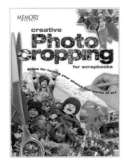

Bibliography & Web Sites

Burns, Robert B. *Child Development: A Text for the Caring Professions.* New York: Nichols Publishing Company. 1986

Furgeson, Lael C. and Stephanie F. Taylor. *Family Scrapbooking.* New York: Sterling Publishing Company. 2000

Ramey, Craig T. *Going to School: How to Help Your Child Succeed.* New York: Goddard Press. 1999

WEB SITES

www.healthleader.uthouston.edu/archive/children/010813 (University of Texas Health Science Center at Houston, *"Plain Sense: Self Esteem"*)

www.plainsense.com/Health/Children/self_esteem.htm

http://ohioline.osu.edu/hyg-fact/5000/5263.html (Ohio State University Fact Sheet, *"Building Children's Self Esteem"*)

Index

A

Activities & special events, 54-87
Adding eyelets, 92
All in a day's work, 34-53
—Blair's story, 39
—Gary's story, 45
—James' story, 44
—Johnny's story, 43
—Theresa's story, 46
Awards & ceremonies, 82-83

B

Back to school, 14-33
—Phyllis' story, 23
—Sabina's story, 18
Back-to-school shopping madness, 16-17
Basic tools & supplies, 8-9
Best-loved books about school, 37
Big uses for small portraits, 90

C

Celebrations, 72-79
Checklists, 13
Clubs & activities, 64-67
Complete page, 12
Create a layout, 10
Crop-n-assemble, 11

D

Documenting the difficult times, 104-105
—Alina's story, 104

E

Enlisting your child's help, 93
Eyelets, adding, 92

F

Field days, 80-81
Field trips, 68-71
—Lindsey's story, 71
Flip-up mini album project, 60

G

Getting started, 8-13
Graduation, 84-87

H

Helping your child build confidence, 106
Heritage photos, working with, 98
Home schooling, 50-53
—Adrian's story, 51
—Amy's story, 53
—Diane's story, 52
—Johnna's story, 50
—Susan's story, 51

I

Identifying classmates technique, 102
Instructions & credits, 125-126
Introduction, 7

J

Journaling, 11
Journaling checklist, 13
Journaling mini album project, 24

L

Lettering patterns & page title ideas, 118-119

M

Memorabilia checklist, 13
Memorabilia, photographing 56, 125
Memorabilia, preserving, 26

P

Page title ideas, 118-119
Paper folding, 94-95
Paper silhouettes technique, 99
Party album, 75
Patterns, 118-124
Performances, 61-63

Photo checklist, 13
Photographing for proper perspective, 17
Photographing memorabilia, 56, 125
Photo mats, enlisting your child's help to make, 93
Pocket pages, 26, 86
Pop-up page, 113
Pop-up pattern, 120
Portrait album, 103
Portraits & milestones, 88-115
—Sarah's story, 97
Preserving memorabilia, 26
Punch art borders, 49
Punch-n-stitch technique, 48

Q

Quotes & sayings, 116-117

R

Relieving first-day jitters, 23
Reproducible page patterns, 122-124

S

Scouting, 65-67
Scrapbooks in the classroom, 111
Source guide, 127
Sports, 56-60
—Chris' story, 59
Sports album, 57
Stamping technique, 22
Stitching stamped images, 38
Student appreciation album, 110-111

T

Teacher appreciation album, 112-113
Teacher gift bag, 113
Timelines, 107

W

Working with heritage photos, 98